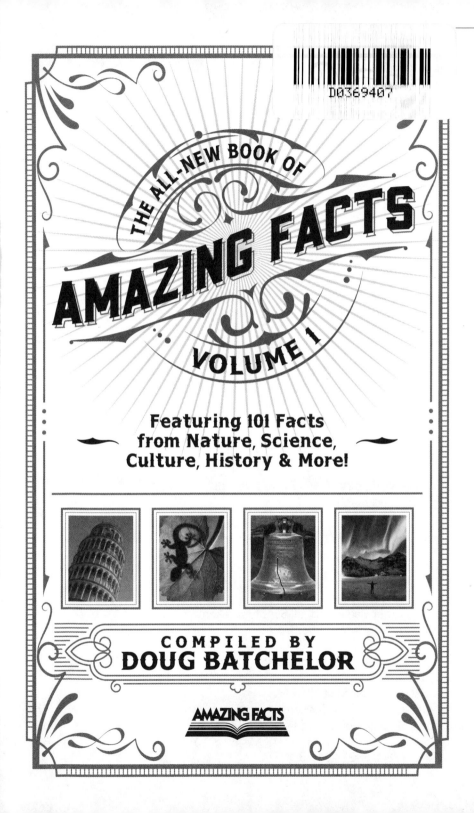

D0369407

THE ALL-NEW BOOK OF

AMAZING FACTS

VOLUME 1

Featuring 101 Facts
from Nature, Science,
Culture, History & More!

COMPILED BY
DOUG BATCHELOR

AMAZING FACTS

The All-New Book of Amazing Facts, Vol. 1
Pastor Doug Batchelor

Copyright 2019 by Amazing Facts, Inc.
P.O. Box 1058
Roseville, CA 95678
afbookstore.com

Unless otherwise noted, all Scripture taken
from the New King James Version.

Project Manager: Anthony Lester
Editor: Laurie Lyon
Assistant Editor: Michelle Kiss
Research: Rosemary McKenzie
Cover design and layout: Haley Trimmer

ISBN: 978-1-58019-641-3

Table of Contents

INTRODUCTION

We are all curious creatures attracted to the extraordinary. I should know; I'm one of them! As a kid, I loved leafing through encyclopedias to learn new and interesting things about our world. Even now, anything out of the ordinary has the potential to capture my attention and stimulate my thinking. Amazing facts are the spice of life!

So it's no surprise that Jesus often used people's natural inquisitiveness as a tool for teaching them, whether through parables about nature or by recalling amazing historic events. This same idea was the basis for Amazing Facts' first radio program, and it's been a staple of my sermons, articles, and *Bible Answers Live* radio program for nearly forty years. In this first volume, I've collected some of my favorite illustrations—old and new—not only to pique your curiosity and entertain you, but also as a resource for exploring Bible truth. I hope this book can be used as a reliable and enjoyable tool for teachers, pastors, and lay evangelists to illustrate the principles of God's Word with fascinating, not-so-typical facts.

Consider the facts herein a savory appetizer to stimulate a deeper hunger for the God who makes infinite wonders.

Doug Batchelor

✑ Editor's Note ✑

Inside this volume, you'll find some of the most eye-opening—and sometimes unbelievable—facts that Pastor Doug has used in his radio and television programs, sermons, and books. Even with our limited resources, we have done our best to ensure the veracity of each and every fact in this volume, vetting them for accuracy and truthfulness. However, if you do spot an inaccuracy along the way, we hope you'll write us to let us know. We'll do our best to make appropriate corrections in future editions.

AMAZING FACTS
Animals &
Biology

⌐ The Human Voice ⌐

Unique in Nature

Yes, the call of a howler monkey can travel three miles and an elephant's vocalization may be deeper—but of all the voices on earth, humans have the most versatile.

Each person's voice uses a marvelous sound-producing mechanism that is more intricate than any musical instrument. Scientists have attempted to reproduce the human voice with computers, but the results often sound unnatural. A human voice can produce a range of octaves by using just two wedge-like projections of ligament and muscle, called vocal cords. These sounds are amplified by built-in resonators in our heads called sinus cavities.

In order to sing a high C, a soprano's vocal cords must vibrate—that is, open and close—1,200 times per second. On the other hand, a bass singer's lowest note requires only 40 vibrations per second.

Besides singing, human voices are capable of producing the most complex variations in speech, with 72 sets of muscles working with split-second timing. In talking for one minute, the tongue, jaw, and lips make at least 300 separate movements. At the same time, our vocal cords vibrate and our respiratory muscles force out just the right amount of air. And if this isn't complex enough, think of the many inflections the voice is capable of producing—ranging up to nearly 500 audible pitches! One can vary tone and volume tremendously, from an ear-ringing shout to a delicate whisper.

But one Man had the most distinct human voice in history—Jesus. *"No man ever spoke like this Man!"* (John 7:46).

— Bamboo —

More Than Mere Gigantic Grass

Did you know that bamboo is a type of grass considered to be the fastest-growing plant in the world? Known for its tall, thick stalks, bamboo is a member of the true grass family known as Poaceae. In the warmer climates of Asia, bamboo can grow as much as 39 inches per day! How would you like to keep that grass mowed?

Bamboo grows so fast, you can actually hear it growing—if you stand in a bamboo forest on a sunny day. There are around 1,500 known species of bamboo, which come in several different colors, such as black, green, gold, gray, red, yellow, and powder blue.

The bamboo plant is also versatile, with an extraordinary range of uses—from garden tools and fishing rods to bird cages and roofing, to name just a few.

In fact, during WWII in the South Pacific, the U.S. Navy used bamboo to reinforce concrete! Pretty incredible when you remember that bamboo is just, well … gigantic grass!

Did you know that the Bible compares man's mortal nature to grass? *"All flesh is as grass, and all the glory of man as the flower of the grass. The grass withers, and its flower falls away, but the word of the LORD endures forever"* (1 Peter 1:24, 25).

⚊ Sponges ⚊

Ancient History

For thousands of years, people have been utilizing freshwater and saltwater sponges in countless ways. For instance, early Europeans used sponges for water filtration, painting, and even helmet padding. However, by the mid-twentieth century, over-harvesting nearly brought soft sponges to extinction. But the invention of synthetic sponges helped turn the tide.

There are more than 7,000 known species of sponges. While they may look like an underwater plant, they are indeed animals. True, they don't have nervous, digestive, or circulatory systems; instead, they depend on constant waterflow through their bodies to obtain food and remove waste. The largest-known species is the giant barrel sponge, which can reach eight feet in height.

Sponges are also some of the longest-living creatures. While turtles and fish do feed on them, if left untouched, sponges can live for centuries. Scientists dated a large sponge found in the Antarctic Ocean to AD 461—that's over 1,550 years old. But one of the larger varieties has been estimated to have lived more than 2,400 years, dating back to before the time of Christ! And did you know that a sponge played a part during the crucifixion of Jesus? *"Jesus, knowing that all things were now accomplished, that the Scripture might be fulfilled, said, 'I thirst!' Now a vessel full of sour wine was sitting there; and they filled a sponge with sour wine, put it on hyssop, and put it to His mouth. So when Jesus had received the sour wine, He said, 'It is finished!' And bowing His head, He gave up His spirit"* (John 19:28–30).

— The Water Spider —
Arachnid Scuba Divers

In Europe, Asia, and parts of Africa, a curious little spider makes its home under water. This water spider spins a tiny web in the shape of a bell and attaches it to the stems of water weeds and plants just below the surface of a freshwater pond.

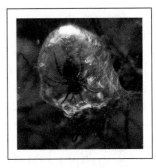

Since all spiders need to breathe air, the water spider takes its air along with it—like a scuba diver. On the surface, it traps tiny bubbles in the hairs of its body, then hurries home and brushes them off, releasing them under its web. The spider makes regular trips to bring back air bubbles for its underwater nest. The waterproof web becomes inflated with trapped air and makes a perfect place to live, eat, and lay eggs.

When the fresh air is used up, the spider returns to the surface to breathe and collect more fresh air bubbles for its home below. Living below, yet breathing the air from above, this little spider is constantly surrounded by water but remains perfectly dry!

Jesus prayed that while His followers were in the world they would be protected, daily breathing in fresh spiritual air from above. *"I do not pray that You should take them out of the world, but that You should keep them from the evil one. They are not of the world, just as I am not of the world"* (John 17:15, 16).

— Bald Eagles —
Unmatched Eye Sight

Among the most unusual of birds, bald eagles primarily eat fish and live up to forty years in the wild. Furthermore, they are monogamous, remaining faithful to their mate until death. But these amazing birds are especially known for their keen eyesight.

Eagles have two foveae, or centers of focus, in the retina of each eye that allow them to see both forward and to the side at the same time. (Human retinas have only one.) Depending on which way the eagle looks, the lens of its eye focuses an image on one fovea or the other. The rear fovea is for forward stereoscopic vision, and the other is for looking sideways. Both foveae are more densely lined with rods and cones than those of human eyes, giving them much greater resolving power.

They also have eyelids that close during sleep. For blinking, they have an inner eyelid called a nictitating membrane. Every three or four seconds, the nictitating membrane slides across the eye from front to back, wiping dirt and dust from the cornea. Because the membrane is translucent, the eagle can see even while the membrane covers the eye.

Eagles have color vision, and while their eyes are not as large as a human's, their sharpness is at least four times that of an individual with perfect vision. While soaring, gliding, or flapping, they are capable of seeing fish in the water from several hundred feet above. An eagle flying in a fixed position at an altitude of 1,000 feet could spot prey as small as a rabbit over an area of almost three square miles!

An eagle's eyes are impressive, but the Creator's eyes see every detail of our lives. *"The LORD is in His holy temple, the LORD's throne is in heaven; His eyes behold, His eyelids test the sons of men"* (Psalm 11:4).

Titan Arum

Big Bad Flower

Normally when we think of flowers, we picture something small, delicate, and fragrant. But those are not words you'd use to describe one flower growing in the rainforests of Sumatra. Known as the "titan arum," this giant flower can take up to ten years to produce its first bloom.

When it does bloom, you'll know it. The flower looks like an eight-foot-long loaf of French bread protruding straight up from the deep burgundy and green-pleated skirt that surrounds its base. One record-breaking specimen in a botanical garden in New Hampshire had a central spike reaching more than 10 feet high and leaves 13 feet around. This plant is also heavy, with some specimens weighing in at over 300 pounds.

The titan arum is also known as the "corpse flower" because it emits a sickening smell. Some have described the odor as a cross between dirty socks, garlic, limburger cheese, and rotten fish. The plant produces the rotten smell for about 48 hours to attract the flies and beetles that help pollinate it.

It's hard to imagine such a large, majestic flower producing such a powerful stench. The Bible says Satan's counterfeits often work the same way—appealing at first, but rotten when one has been deceived by them. *"So the great dragon was cast out, that serpent of old, called the Devil and Satan, who deceives the whole world" (Revelation 12:9).*

Bombardier Beetles

Exploding the Myth

There are more than 400,000 species of beetles on earth, but the bombardier beetle stands out with one of the most incredible defense systems in the natural world. Whenever threatened by an enemy—ants, frogs, and spiders—this spirited little bug shoots a jet of boiling chemicals and irritating, foul-smelling gases at its attacker. From two large glands that open on the tip of its abdomen, this toxic spray explodes right in the face of the unfortunate aggressor.

With some bombardier beetles, you can hear the explosion as a loud pop, which is a result of rapid firing. This rapid-fire action is called "pulse combustion" and jets the boiling liquid at up to 700 pulses per second at 212 degrees Fahrenheit! In addition, the beetle can rotate the end of its abdomen in any direction, like a tiny cannon, and hit the target with great accuracy.

Scientists have learned that the fiery beetle makes its explosive by mixing together two chemicals—hydroquinone and hydrogen peroxide. These chemicals are stored in a reservoir until they're needed. Then, whenever it's approached by a predator, this clever bug squirts a drop of the stored chemicals into each of the two combustion tubes. These tubes contain enzymes that act as the match to create a violent explosion that scorches the poor attacker. For some reason, the beetle is not bothered by the heat and irritation that comes from its own spray.

It is preposterous to believe such a complex mechanism could have evolved piecemeal over millions of years. This would require thousands of generations of these little beetles blowing themselves to pieces.

Did you know that the Bible promises explosive power to those who mix prayer and Bible study? *"You have known the Holy Scriptures, which are able to make you wise for salvation through faith which is in Christ Jesus"* (2 Timothy 3:15).

Bowhead Whale

Huge Bodies, Long Lives

The bowhead whale is a large, stocky, dark-colored leviathan that haunts the fertile Arctic Ocean. It can grow up to 60 feet long and weigh 75 tons, second only to the blue whale in weight. Yet despite its colossal size, it is able to leap entirely out of the water.

Photo credit: Bering Land Bridge National Preserve

Bowhead whales get their name from their massive bow-shaped skull, which is over 16 feet long and accounts for about 40 percent of their total body length. They are also capable of using their humongous noggins to ram through sea ice measuring eighteen inches thick, which is why it's a good thing they also have the thickest blubber of any whale.

Bowheads are able to open their mouths wide enough to park an SUV inside, which seems odd because they survive by feeding on the smallest animals in the ocean—plankton.

One of the most amazing things about bowhead whales concerns their longevity. Based on the recovery of stone harpoon tips in their blubber, and from an analysis of their eye tissue, scientists believe that the lifespan of bowhead whales may be over two hundred years. Science writers from the Geophysical Institute at the University of Alaska Fairbanks have estimated the age of one bowhead whale at 211 years! This would make it the oldest known mammal that exists, and it means there probably are bowhead whales swimming around that were alive when Abraham Lincoln was president.

We may envy animals with long lives, but God has promised His people life that lasts forever! *"These things I have written to you who believe in the name of the Son of God, that you may know that you have eternal life" (1 John 5:13).*

Bristlecone Pine
Made for Tribulation

The bristlecone pine, a Great Basin tree, can live more than four thousand years. One estimated at nearly 5,000 years old is believed to be among the oldest living trees on the planet. This tree was around when the Egyptians were building the pyramids!

Some of these ancient evergreens found on lonely mountain tops have weathered thousands of years of intense freezing wind, pounding rain, scorching sun, and violent electrical storms. How have they managed to survive through millennia of such adverse weather? Their root system is highly branched and shallow, while their wood is dense and resinous.

Jesus foretold that there will be a time of trouble coming upon the world just before His return—unlike anything in history. This tribulation will be so intense and frightening that if it were not cut short, no life on earth would survive. *"For then there will be great tribulation, such as has not been since the beginning of the world until this time, no, nor ever shall be. And unless those days were shortened, no flesh would be saved; but for the elect's sake those days will be shortened"* (Matthew 24:21, 22).

Bumblebees

Humble Flyers

Once called "humblebees" because of their good nature, bumblebees rarely have it in them to sting. The name "bumblebee" was first introduced to the English language in 1530, but it was popularized in a children's book in the early 1900s. Since World War II, the use of "humblebee" has declined dramatically.

Worldwide, there are over 250 different species of bumblebees. These round, fuzzy, nectar-loving insects are found mostly in the Northern Hemisphere and in South America.

Bumblebees are among the few insects that can control their body temperature. In cold weather, queens and workers can shiver their flight muscles to warm themselves. Their large size and heat-conserving hairy coats also help them stay warm, allowing them to fly and work in colder climates and lower temperatures than most other insects.

Entomologist Antoine Magnan once mused that with small wings and fat bodies, it should be aerodynamically difficult for bumblebees to fly. Of course, the bumblebees haven't had time to read any reports (no, they don't violate physics), so they continue doing what God designed them to do. *"I can do all things through Christ who strengthens me" (Philippians 4:13).*

Coelacanth

Living Fossil

In December 1938, a strange fish was caught in a net near the mouth of the Chalumna River in South Africa. Captain Hendrik Goosen thought the fish was bizarre enough to alert the local museum in the small town of East London.

The museum's director, Miss Marjorie Courtney-Latimer, described the creature as "the most beautiful fish I had ever seen, five feet long, and a pale mauve blue with iridescent silver markings."

Searching through the few reference books on hand, Marjorie found a picture that led her to a seemingly impossible conclusion: Her specimen bore striking similarities to a long-extinct prehistoric fish! The prominent South African ichthyologist Dr. J. L. B. Smith was alerted to this amazing discovery. The professor came at once and identified the fish as a coelacanth (sê-le-kànth´). The fish would soon be called the "most important zoological find of the century." They had discovered a living fossil.

This particular species of fish was firmly believed to have lived long before the time of the dinosaurs, with the fossil record dating them back more than 360 million years. They were thought to have gone extinct around the same time as the dinosaurs—about 65 million years ago. Dr. Smith, Miss Courtney-Latimer, and the coelacanth became overnight celebrities. When a one-day-only public viewing was arranged, 20,000 visitors showed up. Since then, several other coelacanths have been caught, mostly around Indonesia.

How could the coelacanth supposedly disappear for more than 80 million years and then turn up alive and well in the twentieth century? It had also been taught that the coelacanth was a "missing link" with its "proto legs" that were supposedly evolving into limbs. Yet if the theory of evolution is true and these fish have been around since before the dinosaurs, then why have they not evolved any further? *"For in six days the Lord made the heavens and the earth, the sea, and all that is in them" (Exodus 20.11).*

Dogs
Amazing Noses

Did you know that the part of a dog's brain devoted to analyzing smells is, proportionally speaking, forty times greater than ours? That's why dogs are trained to search and rescue people after avalanches, earthquakes, and mudslides. The average dog's nose is tens of thousands of times as sensitive to odors as ours.

For comparison, if we were to illustrate this by using the sense of vision, what humans could see at one-third of a mile, a dog could see more clearly three thousand miles away! Put another way, dogs can detect some odors in parts per trillion. While we might notice a teaspoon of sugar added to our lemonade, a dog could detect a teaspoon of sugar in a million gallons of water—the equivalent of two Olympic-sized pools.

Experts have reported incredible stories of drug-sniffing dogs that located marijuana in a plastic container submerged in gasoline within a gas tank. Then there's the cancer-sniffing dog that can detect a microscopic spot of melanoma on a patient's skin. While a dog may not always "smell pretty," their sense of smell is pretty amazing!

Did you know that the Bible talks about a man who was deceived through his sense of smell? *"Then his father Isaac said to him, 'Come near now and kiss me, my son.' And he came near and kissed him; and he smelled the smell of his clothing, and blessed him"* (Genesis 27:26, 27).

Elephants
Hunted Toward Extinction

Throughout history, elephants have been revered for their size and strength. They have been trained to trample enemies on the battlefield and to haul heavy supplies through jungles. As the world's largest land animal, a full-grown African elephant can weigh more than 10,000 pounds. As vegetarians, they must consume as much as 300 pounds of food per day.

The most famous characteristic of elephants is their trunk, which is really nothing more than an elongation of the nose and upper lip. Still, it is amazingly versatile. Composed of an estimated 150,000 muscles, the trunk is employed as a nose, arm, hand, and otherwise multipurpose tool to pull branches off trees, uproot grass, pluck fruit, and to place food in their mouths. It's also used for smelling, trumpeting, drinking, greeting, or throwing dirt for a dust bath. When in deep water, elephants hold their trunks above the water like snorkels.

Elephant tusks are elongated upper incisors and are the largest and heaviest teeth of any living animal. They are used for digging for roots and water, stripping the bark off trees for food, and as a defense against predators. Tusks grow continuously throughout an elephant's life, growing up to 10 feet and weighing as much as 200 pounds each. This ivory, also known as "white gold," was used at one time in the manufacture of piano keys, billiard balls, and other objects. Over the years, hunters have slaughtered thousands of these magnificent animals just for their tusks. At the turn of the twentieth century, elephants numbered from five to ten million, but widespread hunting and habitat destruction reduced their numbers to an estimated 600,000.

Did you know the Bible predicts that in the last days, Christians will be hunted because they choose to obey God's commandments? *"The dragon was enraged with the woman, and he went to make war with the rest of her offspring, who keep the commandments of God and have the testimony of Jesus Christ" (Revelation 12:17).*

European Cuckoo

The Brood Parasite

Known as a "brood parasite," the female European cuckoo lays her eggs in the nests of smaller bird species—such as the reed warbler. In turn, these unsuspecting mothers unwittingly incubate, feed, and raise the young imposters, typically at the expense of their own offspring.

The cuckoo's appearance, similar to a sparrowhawk, temporarily frightens away the host bird, which gives the cuckoo a chance to secretly lay its eggs in the host nest. One of the tragedies of nature is when a little reed warbler works itself to death to satisfy the voracious appetite of a fat cuckoo chick, while her own starving young are crowded out of the nest!

Many don't realize that the devil has laid an egg in the Christian church that has been hatched, adopted, and fed until it has grown bigger than life. *"But there were also false prophets among the people, even as there will be false teachers among you, who will secretly bring in destructive heresies" (2 Peter 2:1).*

Geckos
Sticky Feet

Geckos are small, insect-eating lizards that have a miraculous ability to scurry up walls and stick to ceilings. Back in the fourth century BC, Aristotle noted their amazing climbing abilities, and scientists have been wondering ever since how these creatures can walk up smooth surfaces or even upside down on polished glass.

Researchers now think they may have solved the riddle. Geckos' sticky ability appears to come from a weak magnetic attraction that molecules have for one another. Looking through a microscope reveals fine hairs, or "setae," on each of their toes. The end of each hair is further subdivided into hundreds of structures called "spatulae." These spatulae, which look like broccoli, produce electrical attractions that are pressed so close to a surface they "electrically glue" the animal to the surface.

A team of biologists and engineers calculated the combined adhesive force of all the tiny hairs lining the gecko's toes at ten times greater than the maximum force needed to pull a gecko off the wall. (It is estimated that if our feet had the same "sticking power," each foot could hold about 90 pounds to a glass ceiling.) The gecko hairs have also been shown to be self-cleaning, unlike any other known adhesive. Geckos have also developed an amazing way of walking: They scamper up walls and across ceilings by rolling these hairs onto the surface and then peeling them off again, just like tape, all within a fraction of a second.

The Bible talks about this kind of "sticking power" or adhesive force in marriage—giving clear instruction that when a man finds a wife, he is to leave his father and mother and cleave to his wife. "*A wife is not to depart from her husband. ... And a husband is not to divorce his wife*" (1 Corinthians 7:10, 11).

Giraffes

The Leopard Camel

Among land animals, giraffes stand head and shoulders above the rest—towering up to 18 feet. Giraffes are herbivores, and their extended neck, combined with their 18-inch long tongue, allows them to reach the tasty leaves high in the tall, thorny acacia trees.

Although the giraffe's neck is about seven feet long, it contains the same number of vertebrae as a mouse—seven; of course, each vertebra is greatly elongated. In fact, every time a giraffe picks up its neck, it raises about 600 pounds! Its circulatory system is specially adapted for its long neck. They have elastic blood vessels in the neck and head to handle changes in blood pressure due to head swings. This is why a giraffe's heart must weigh a whopping 25 pounds to pump the blood to such a high altitude!

With each step, a giraffe travels about 15 feet. They are also fast runners and can reach speeds of 37 mph—the average speed of a Kentucky Derby racehorse. Though male giraffes will often "neck wrestle" to establish dominance, they are generally passive, non-territorial, and sociable. They live in loose, open herds grazing peacefully with zebra, wildebeest, and antelope.

Julius Caesar brought the first giraffe ever seen in the West to Rome in about 46 BC. Because they are as big as a camel with spots like a leopard, they were thought to be the result of a freakish breeding of the two animals. Although we know that the giraffe is not a combination of these two animals, the scientific name "Camelopardalis" stuck.

We might laugh at the gullible Romans who believed you could combine a camel with a leopard—but the bigger question is: How can a being be fully God and fully man? *"For there is one God and one Mediator between God and men, the Man Christ Jesus" (1 Timothy 2:5).*

Hammer Orchid

Masterful Mimicry

Most plants and flowers must pollinate to survive, so the Lord has devised many ingenious ways to help them spread these precious particles of life. Wind is the most common, but there are also the birds, the bees, and even some mammals that assist with pollination.

Photo credit: Brundrm

Some orchids, however, achieve pollination by offering the promise of marriage. Parts of the flower are designed to resemble the female versions of certain insects, and the imitation is astounding. Take, for example, the Australian hammer orchid, which takes advantage of a mating ritual of the thynnid wasp. The lower lip of the hammer orchid's flower mimics a female wasp resting on a twig looking upward, just waiting for a male flying by to spot her. Even to the human eye, it almost perfectly resembles the plump, wingless female wasp, complete with a shiny head and furry body. The orchid even releases an enticing female wasp pheromone—a chemical copy of the same perfume the female wasp wears. Poised at the end of an arm just above this alluring decoy are sticky bags filled with pollen.

A male thynnid wasp flying by, lured by the imitation scent, will grab the decoy and try to fly off with "her" in his grasp. As he takes off, however, his momentum flips him and his flowery pretender up and over, right into the sticky pollen sacks. After realizing his mistake, he releases the decoy—and flies off, only to be fooled again by another hammer orchid that he now pollinates with the pollen he picked up on his previous bad date.

When real female thynnid wasps are around, males will invariably choose a live one over the impostor. God conveniently designed these orchids to bloom in the brief period several weeks before the female wasps emerge from underground—giving the flower a temporary advantage when male wasps are flying but females are not around.

Mimicry in nature is truly remarkable, even humorous, but a wolf in sheep's clothes is no laughing matter when it comes to our souls. *"Beware of false prophets, who come to you in sheep's clothing, but inwardly they are ravenous wolves" (Matthew 7:15).*

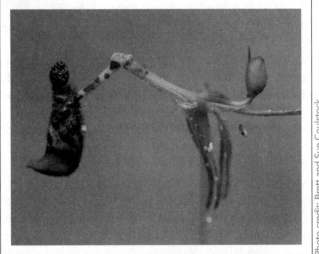

Photo credit: Brett and Sue Coulstock

Crows and Ravens

Bird Brains

We don't usually think of birds as being intelligent. After all, that's where we get the expression "bird-brain." But crows are an exception. Researchers believe their clever, witty behavior ranks their intelligence with that of dogs and even chimps.

Found just about everywhere in the world, crows adapt well to almost any environment. Their omnivorous diet helps them thrive in cities and suburban areas. Crows demonstrate sophisticated social behavior, playing tricks on each other and fabricating tools to get food. One crow was videotaped using leverage to bend a straight piece of wire into a hook. He then used the hook to fish a bucket of food from a deep tube. No other animal—not even a chimp—has ever been witnessed solving a problem like this spontaneously.

Crows mate for life and are protective of their young. Perhaps you have even seen them "dive bomb" people or animals if they approach too close to their nest. The world's longest-living crow, named Tata, died in July 2006. As a fledgling, Tata was blown from her nest in a Long Island cemetery during a fierce thunderstorm. The baby crow with a broken wing was adopted by a local family. That was back in 1947. Tata never did learn to fly, but that might be one reason she lived 59 years.

Ravens are closely related to crows but are 30 percent bigger, and they also have among the largest brains of any bird. They typically live about 15 years in the wild, although lifespans of up to 40 years have been recorded.

You might be interested to know that ravens are the first birds mentioned in the Bible. And did you know the Bible states that ravens can teach us about putting our trust in God? *"Consider the ravens, for they neither sow nor reap, which have neither storehouse nor barn; and God feeds them. Of how much more value are you than the birds?" (Luke 12:24).*

Kangaroos

Amazing Marsupials

Kangaroos are among the most unique creatures on God's earth. Different species of them can be found living all over Australia—from big open plains and deserts to forests. Fossils tell us Australia once had kangaroos ten feet tall. Today, the red kangaroo is the world's largest marsupial, growing to six feet and weighing as much as 200 pounds. It can also run nearly 40 mph, bounding in arcs 10 feet high and 25 feet across!

Kangaroos are the only large animals that move by hopping. Their strong tails are used for balance when hopping and as a fifth limb when grazing. All kangaroos are herbivores, and those living in the drier regions need very little water. Red kangaroos can even go without water if fresh grass is available.

But these vegetarians can be deadly. The powerful hind legs—with their long, sharp toenails—are a dangerous weapon. With one kick, kangaroos can disembowel opponents.

A doe kangaroo can become pregnant again directly after a joey is born, but the development of that pregnancy will be suspended until the first baby is lost or leaves the pouch. This means a female kangaroo can have three babies at the same time: an older joey living outside the pouch, a young one in the pouch, and an embryo on hold.

It's also fascinating that the doe is able to develop two kinds of milk to feed her two nursing offspring—a high-fat milk for the younger joey in the pouch and a high-carbohydrate milk for the older joey. But, eventually, the young kangaroos must learn to live off solid food.

Did you know that the Bible says some baby Christians never get weaned? *"Though by this time you ought to be teachers, you need someone to teach you again the first principles of the oracles of God; and you have come to need milk and not solid food. For everyone who partakes only of milk is unskilled in the word of righteousness"* (Hebrews 5:12, 13).

Ants
A Colony that Works

Ants are believed to be the most numerous creatures on earth. Supposedly, the combined weight of all ants is greater than the combined weight of all humans, making up one-tenth of the world's total volume of animal tissue.

Strong in relation to their size, most ants can carry ten to twenty times their body weight and work in teams to move extremely heavy things. And if a man could run proportionally as fast as an ant, he could run as fast as a racehorse.

The ant's mushroom-shaped brain contains about 250,000 brain cells and functions similar to human brains, which have 100 billion cells. Extremely social, ants also share these activities with humans:

- Livestock Farming: Ants herd aphids like sheep and "milk" them for nectar-like food.

- Cultivation: They grow underground gardens for food.

- Child Care: They tenderly feed young and provide intensive nursery care, all while maintaining a careful climate control for developing ants.

- Civic Duties: They respond and organize for massive group projects.

- Military Forces: Ants raise an army of specialized soldiers to ward off insects, animals, and other threats.

- Flood Control: They incorporate water traps to keep out rain.

- Communications: Ants have a complex tactile and chemical communication system.

- Career Specialization: Some clean, some forage, some care for the young, and some are guards or scouts.

But as intelligent and resourceful as they are, ants cannot survive alone. They can only exist and thrive as part of a colony. The Bible teaches that Christians too will thrive only as part of a church family. *"As the body is one and has many members, but all the members of that one body, being many, are one body, so also is Christ"* (1 Corinthians 12:12).

Moses and Cassie

The Crow and the Kitten

One day in 1999, Wallace and Ann Collito found a tiny black-and-white kitten in their backyard. This older couple believed someone might have tossed the kitten over the fence that surrounded their mobile home park, and they were concerned for the helpless little creature—until they noticed that a crow had stepped in to babysit the kitten.

Stock photo illustration

The Collitos began to feed the small waif, but as they watched each day, they were amazed to see that the bird, which they named Moses, stayed close by and was actually feeding the kitten, which they named Cassie. Moses not only found bugs and worms and poked them into the cat's mouth, but he also guarded her against other animals and tried to keep her from going into the street by flapping his wings and cawing vigorously. He was a great protector.

Because the Collitos guessed that no one would ever believe their incredible story without proof, they filmed and photographed the two animals interacting and playing together.

Did you know the Bible says God used crows to care for His people? *"The word of the LORD came to him, saying, 'Get away from here and turn eastward, and hide by the Brook Cherith, which flows into the Jordan. And it will be that you shall drink from the brook, and I have commanded the ravens to feed you there.' … The ravens brought him bread and meat in the morning, and bread and meat in the evening; and he drank from the brook"* (1 Kings 17:2–4, 6).

Matriphagy
The Ultimate Sacrifice

Matriphagy is a rare behavior, more commonly found in spiders, in which a creature feeds on its own mother. Most mothers would do *anything* for their children. In the case of some arachnid mothers, like the velvet desert spider, they make the ultimate sacrifice for their young. They offer themselves as prey to their offspring as an essential last step to awaken their hunting instincts and provide a meal.

Photo credit: Sarefo

At first, the baby spiders feed on a milk-like liquid the mother excretes. When she eventually runs out of milk, the mother circles the youngsters, tapping and vibrating the web, calling in the 50 to 80 starving spiderlings. The baby spiders swarm in a frenzy, somehow aware that when the web vibrates, it's time to eat.

The mother then presses herself into her babies, offering herself as a feast. She makes no attempt to escape as her young eventually pierce her soft abdomen with their mouths and gradually devour her.

Did you know the Bible talks about a parent who offered His body as a sacrifice so His children could survive? *"Then Jesus said to them, 'Most assuredly, I say to you, unless you eat the flesh of the Son of Man and drink His blood, you have no life in you. Whoever eats My flesh and drinks My blood has eternal life, and I will raise him up at the last day' "* (John 6:53, 54).

Migration
The Internal Compass

How do animals know when it's time to migrate? And how do they find their way back to the same beach, stream, or feeding ground they've not seen since birth?

Consider the green turtles that swim from their feeding grounds off the coast of Brazil to tiny Ascension Island—1,200 miles away—which they have not visited since they were hatched.

The Chinook salmon migrates farther than any other salmon, traveling up to 2,000 miles inland to spawn in the exact freshwater streams as did their ancestors.

The monarch butterfly is known for its extraordinarily long migrations, which it makes twice in its two-year lifespan. During the summer months, millions of monarchs can be found fluttering from Canada and the United States to their winter home in central Mexico—traveling in some cases more than 2,000 miles.

And an estimated 10 billion birds engage in migratory flights annually. One species of shrike wings its way 3,500 miles from Central Asia to the Equator of Africa. The longest flight made by a homing pigeon was in 1931 from Arras, France, to Saigon, Vietnam. To demonstrate that homing pigeons are not guided by landmarks, the feisty fowl was taken to France in a covered cage aboard a ship. When released, the pigeon flew straight as an arrow 7,200 miles over unfamiliar land to its home in only 24 days.

But the Arctic tern has the longest migration of any animal. Winging each year from their nesting grounds in the Arctic North to the Antarctic and back, terns make a round-trip journey of nearly 25,000 miles!

It seems God has also placed this inner drive to migrate in many of His other creatures, but only when He has established a place for them to go. *"You in Your mercy have led forth the people whom You have redeemed; You have guided them in Your strength to Your holy habitation"* (Exodus 15:13).

Two-Headed Turtle

A Split Personality

In 2013, a two-headed turtle was born at the San Antonio Zoo. Although being in captivity gave the turtle its best chance of survival, it stopped growing at a young age and died at just over a year old.

Stock photo illustration

Each head of the turtle was different; each had its own brain and personality. One side was very curious, while the other was much more aggressive.

According to scientists, two-headedness can occur in all animals, but the lifespan is typically short. The reason is because each head tends to work independently of the other, controlling its own side of the body, and therefore creating disunity, confusion, and frustration. Unless one head takes primary control, the creature will soon die from starvation and indecision.

When we're tempted, it may sometimes seem like we have two competing heads—one that wants to give in to the temptation and one that resists.

Many believe it is a sin to be tempted. This is not true. Jesus was tempted in the wilderness, so it can't possibly be a sin to be tempted. Rather, it is a sin to give in to temptation. *"For we do not have a High Priest who cannot sympathize with our weaknesses, but was in all points tempted as we are, yet without sin"* (Hebrews 4:15).

Rabbit-Proof Fence
Mass Migration

When Dutch explorers first discovered Australia in 1606, there were no rabbits to be found throughout the continent. That all changed in 1859, when an English settler, Thomas Austin, released 24 rabbits on his property near Melbourne, Australia.

While living in England, Austin loved hunting rabbits for sport. At the time, he thought the introduction of a few rabbits could do little harm and might provide a touch of home. As we know, rabbits are extremely prolific creatures. And with Australia's mild winters, Austin's rabbits were able to breed year-round. Along with plentiful vegetation, this provided the perfect conditions for a rabbit population explosion.

Within ten years of their introduction, rabbits had become so prevalent that two million could be shot or trapped annually without making a noteworthy dent in their numbers. It was the fastest spread ever recorded in history of any mammal anywhere in the world. In a desperate attempt to halt the spread of rabbits to Western Australia, the country built what they hoped would be a Rabbit-Proof Fence.

Beginning in 1901, the fence took six years to build. When completed in 1907, it was the longest fence in the world, stretching more than 2,000 miles from north to south. But the fence did not stop the rabbits from migrating westward. The rabbits tunneled their way under eroded sections of the fence, jumped through holes in the damaged wire, and other times they simply hopped through gates that were accidentally left open. Today, rabbits are entrenched in Australia and number in the hundreds of millions.

Did you know the Bible speaks of an unstoppable population explosion and mass migration? The Bible says when the children of Israel entered Egypt, there were 70 people. When they left during the Exodus 215 years later, there were 603,550 males aged between 20 and 60. If you do the math, there must have been around 2 to 2.5

million Israelites! *"The children of Israel were fruitful and increased abundantly, multiplied and grew exceedingly mighty; and the land was filled with them. ... But the more they afflicted them, the more they multiplied and grew"* (Exodus 1:7, 12).

Rocky Mountain Locust

Super Swarms

The Rocky Mountain locust was an abundant species of grasshopper that ranged through regions of North America until the late 1800s. Sightings of swarms were often reported in numbers far larger than any other species of locust in the world, including one famous swarm in 1875 that blackened the sky for five days in several states.

This super-swarm consumed fields like a prairie fire, causing a famine in the Midwest. This locust swarm of biblical proportions was estimated to be 110 miles wide and 1,800 miles long. That comes to about 198,000 square miles in size—a super-organism larger than the state of California and weighing over 27 million tons.

According to Guinness World Records, this swarm consisted of approximately 12 trillion insects and was the greatest concentration of creatures ever reported.

Incredibly, less than 30 years later, the Rocky Mountain locust was extinct. The last recorded sighting of a live specimen was in 1902 in southern Canada. It is believed the historic wave of settlers sweeping across the west inadvertently plowed up the locusts' favorite locations for breeding and laying eggs.

The Bible records that plagues of locusts were often followed by famines, and Jesus warned us that there will be pestilences and famines in the last days. *"And there will be great earthquakes in various places, and famines and pestilences" (Luke 21:11).*

The Human Tongue
A Dangerous Muscle

Did you know that the tongue is almost all muscle? It features muscle fibers that run vertically, transversely, and longitudinally—allowing great range of motion. As a result, it's capable of very precise, complicated, and elaborate movements.

It also has many important responsibilities that we tend to take for granted. For instance, the tongue is necessary for speech—no matter what language. Without a tongue, there would be no talking, no singing, and no whistling.

The tongue is also vital for eating. The upper surface is covered with small projections, called papilla, that give it a rough texture. This design helps the tongue move food around in the mouth and direct it to your throat. Without your tongue, you would have to lay back to eat.

The tongue is also the source of one of your most favorite senses—taste! It is covered with approximately 10,000 taste buds that are sensitive to sweet, sour, salty, and bitter flavors. Chemicals from the food we eat stimulate receptors in each of these areas, and nerves transmit this input to the brain.

Life would be pretty dull without a tongue. Imagine food with no taste! The tongue does get a lot of recognition; we often hear phrases like tongue-in-cheek, tongue tied, and tongue twister. But the Bible says the tongue can also be dangerous, and it would be best for us to stop this muscle from doing wrong. *"Keep your tongue from evil, and your lips from speaking deceit" (Psalm 34:13).*

The Manchineel
Tree of Death

Among the tropical beaches in the Gulf of Mexico, you can find a harmless looking tree with sweet-smelling fruits that look like crabapples. But this is one apple in paradise you do not want to eat. Indeed, even a single bite can cause hours of agony—and potentially death.

According to Guinness World Records, the manchineel tree is the most dangerous tree in the world. When eaten, the fruit is reported to be pleasantly sweet at first, with a subsequent strange peppery feeling. Gradually, this progresses to a burning sensation and tightness in the throat, followed by terrible gastronomical problems. Symptoms continue to worsen until the patient can barely swallow solid food because of the excruciating pain and swelling in the throat.

Every part of the tree is toxic. Manchineel trees are so poisonous that even standing under one in the rain can cause your skin to blister, and the smoke from burning any part of the tree can injure the eyes. Spanish explorer Juan Ponce de León died after being struck by an arrow that had been poisoned with manchineel sap. We can understand why the Spanish call it *arbol de la muerte*, which means "tree of death."

Did you know the Bible also speaks about a tree of death and a tree of life? *"The tree of life was also in the midst of the garden, and the tree of the knowledge of good and evil. … And the Lord God commanded the man, saying, 'Of every tree of the garden you may freely eat; but of the tree of the knowledge of good and evil you shall not eat, for in the day that you eat of it you shall surely die' "* (Genesis 2:9, 16, 17).

Tyrian Purple
The Imperial Dye

Also known as imperial dye, Tyrian purple was a very rare and ancient natural dye. This costly substance came from a secretion produced by Murex sea snails, which are found among coastal rocks around the eastern Mediterranean.

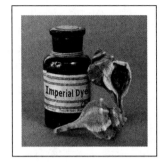

Tyrian purple got the first part of its name because it was popular among the ancient Phoenicians around the city of Tyre. The dye was prized in antiquity because the color was hard to produce and did not fade. In fact, it became even brighter with weathering and sunlight.

The Murex sea snails secrete a mucous substance when they are crushed. It was discovered through testing that 12,000 snails would yield only 1.4 grams of pure purple dye, just enough to color the trim of a single garment. That means almost four million Murex snails were required to make one pound of Tyrian purple. This is why the substance was traded by the ounce, fetching more than silver or gold.

Because Tyrian purple was so expensive, textiles in this color were status symbols tightly controlled in Byzantium. The production of Tyrian purple was eventually subsidized by the government, which restricted its use for only imperial silks. That's why a child born to a reigning emperor was said to be "born in the purple."

Did you know the Bible tells us there was another dye even more expensive than Tyrian purple? *"So he said to me, 'These are the ones who come out of the great tribulation, and washed their robes and made them white in the blood of the Lamb' "* (Revelation 7:14, 15).

Woolly Bear Caterpillars

Amazing Transformation

The Arctic woolly bear caterpillars, found in the far north around Greenland and Canada, are known for their incredible metabolism. They're called "woolly bears" because of their fuzzy brown and black appearance.

After the woolly bear emerges from its egg in the fall, it eats to fatten up until the weather gets too cold. The caterpillar will then crawl under a rock, where it freezes solid through the long arctic winter. In the spring, however, it thaws out, twitches back to life, and starts eating again. It survives being frozen by producing a cryoprotectant antifreeze within its tissues.

In warmer climates, caterpillars are normally voracious eaters that can increase their body mass a thousand times in just a few weeks before becoming moths or butterflies. But in the Arctic, the summers are short and vegetation is sparse, so woolly bears must relentlessly feed through several summers, freezing each winter and thawing out again until they get enough body mass to spin a cocoon and turn into an Isabella tiger moth.

This means woolly bears have the longest lifecycle of any other butterfly or moth. In their journey from egg to wings, some are known to live through as many as 14 winters, surviving temperatures as cold as 60 degrees below zero year after year.

If you've ever felt like you are trapped on a treadmill in your walk with the Lord, just waiting for your wings, remember that He is transforming you as you focus on Him. *"But we all, with unveiled face, beholding as in a mirror the glory of the Lord, are being transformed into the same image from glory to glory, just as by the Spirit of the Lord" (2 Corinthians 3:18).*

AMAZING FACTS

People
& Places

Nan Aspinwall

The Long Rider

Nan Aspinwall was an extraordinary woman who worked as a sharp-shooter, stunt rider, and trick-roper in Buffalo Bill's Wild West Show. Also known as "Two-Gun Nan," this consummate cowgirl with the beauty of a model and ferocious determination accomplished a feat that has never been matched.

According to the story, Bill Cody had a strong disagreement with a rival showman who bet Buffalo Bill that a woman could not complete a transcontinental horse ride alone. Determined to accept the challenge, 31-year-old Nan set off on September 1, 1910. Mounting her mare, Lady Ellen, the intrepid cowgirl picked up a letter from the Mayor of San Francisco addressed to the mayor of New York City and set out on the lonely, arduous journey to deliver the mail.

Over the next 180 days, she covered 4,496 miles alone. Riding 25 to 30 miles a day, Nan had many adventures while crossing mountains and forging rivers, even shoeing her horse by herself 14 times along the way. She packed a pistol and was not afraid to use it. In one place, she sent several bullets into the door of an establishment that was refusing her service. Another time, she spent a week in a hospital after her horse stumbled down a mountainside.

On July 9, 1911, she rode into New York City and delivered her letter to City Hall, becoming the first and only woman to cross the United States by horseback alone.

Did you know the book of Revelation pictures Jesus riding across the heavens on a white horse? *"Now I saw heaven opened, and behold, a white horse. And He who sat on him was called Faithful and True, and in righteousness He judges and makes war"* (Revelation 19:11).

Polyglot
Masters of Human Language

A polyglot is a person who speaks at least six languages and often more. For example, Queen Elizabeth I of England could speak ten languages, and one ambassador claimed she could speak them as though they were her mother tongue.

According to the 2008 *Guinness Book of World Records*, the most prolific polyglot alive today is Ziad Fazah, raised in Beirut and now living in Brazil. He claims he can speak and read 59 languages—including French, English, Spanish, Hindi, Swedish, Swahili, German, Urdu, Chinese, and Russian. According to Fazah, a Christian, his remarkable ability to learn languages is a gift from God.

Did you know the Bible says the Holy Spirit can teach a person an entire language in just a matter of minutes? *"When the Day of Pentecost had fully come, they were all with one accord in one place. ... And they were all filled with the Holy Spirit and began to speak with other tongues, as the Spirit gave them utterance"* (Acts 2:1, 4).

Babylon

Spiritual Lessons

The nation most often mentioned in the Bible is Israel. But do you know which nation is second? It is the area known today as Iraq. Sometimes called the cradle of civilization, the names used in the Bible for this region are Babylon, Land of Shinar, Mesopotamia, and Nineveh. Many Bible characters including Esther, Jonah, Daniel, and Ezekiel were stationed in this historic land.

On two occasions, the people of God were carried off to this land. The ten tribes were carried off into Assyria in 722 BC, and then Nebuchadnezzar destroyed Jerusalem in 587 BC and drove the inhabitants of Judah into 70 years of captivity.

This is one reason Saddam Hussein revered king Nebuchadnezzar; he longed to duplicate the feat of conquering Israel and ruling the Arab nations. Hussein even had himself photographed in a replica of Nebuchadnezzar's war chariot, trying to convince people he was the reincarnation of the ancient king of Babylon.

History later records that Babylon was conquered by the Persians and then the Greeks, but after the death of Alexander, the city began to fade. Ultimately, it ceased to be inhabited and its ruins were swallowed up by the Euphrates River and the shifting sands of the desert.

Many Christians believe that Babylon must be rebuilt before the last events of prophecy can be fulfilled. But the prophet Isaiah promised that nobody would ever live there again—that it would be just a habitation for foxes and owls (Isaiah 13:20, 21). Hussein desperately wanted to prove the Jewish prophet wrong and spent millions in an attempt to rebuild the ruins of Babylon, but his grand plans were thwarted by war and capture. Today, Babylon remains a ghost town.

If the Bible says Babylon will never be rebuilt, then what is the last-day Babylon that is spoken of in the book of Revelation?

"Another angel followed, saying, 'Babylon is fallen, is fallen, that great city, because she has made all nations drink of the wine of the wrath of her fornication' " (Revelation 14:8).

Koshe Rubbish Landfill

Avalanche of Garbage

A tragic landslide in 2017 killed well over one hundred people near Addis Ababa, Ethiopia. When the death toll reached 113, at least another 80 people were still missing. Landslides rarely kill people in Ethiopia; however, this was not your typical landslide of dirt or mud—but rather a landslide of garbage.

The Koshe Rubbish Landfill on the outskirts of Addis Ababa has been a dumping ground for the nation's capital for more than fifty years. Each year, almost 300,000 tons of waste are piled upon this mountain of refuse. Every day, as mobs of crows circle overhead, about 500 people sift through the apocalypse of stinking rubbish looking for anything they may be able to scavenge and sell.

Over time, these poor scavengers had built homes of mud and sticks directly against the ever-growing mountain of trash. Many of these makeshift homes and their occupants were buried by the massive avalanche of rubbish just outside the Ethiopian capital.

How does a person escape a looming mountain of garbage that threatens their spiritual life? *"He will again have compassion on us, and will subdue our iniquities. You will cast all our sins into the depths of the sea"* (Micah 7:19).

Pu'uhonua

City of Refuge

On the largest island in Hawaii, ancient ruins of a village stand with a large oblong temple and a wall 1,000 feet long. The wall was built from 1,550 chunks of lava and measures 18 feet thick at the base and stands 12 feet high. This temple village was called "Pu'uhonua"—or the City of Refuge.

In ancient times, when a native Hawaiian broke one of the "kapu," or sacred laws, he was sentenced to death unless he could flee to this village. Once inside the walls of the village, he was safe and protected from judgment. Later, a priest would perform a rite of purification for the guilty party. He could then be declared forgiven, innocent, and was free to begin a new life.

Jesus is the place of refuge for anyone who desires to be saved, to receive forgiveness for their sins, and to start a new life. *"He has delivered us from the power of darkness and conveyed us into the kingdom of the Son of His love, in whom we have redemption through His blood, the forgiveness of sins" (Colossians 1:13, 14).*

City of the Dead

Life in a Cemetery

One of the strangest cemeteries is found in northern Cairo. It's called the "City of the Dead." The word "cemetery" is actually a misnomer, because this graveyard is teeming with life and activity. For hundreds of years, great Egyptian rulers of ages past built acres and acres of huge and elaborate mausoleums and tombs.

Around the fourteenth century, due to lack of space, thousands of poor and homeless people seeking shelter began squatting in these tombs. Strangely, this cemetery is now classified as a suburb of Cairo. It has its own post office, police station, shops, electricity, running water, and clinics. Today, it is estimated that nearly a million people call this "cemetery" home.

The residents have made creative use of the smaller gravestones by turning them into washing lines or tables. People actually live and conduct their lives in these tombs—sleeping, cooking, and eating—surrounded by their silent macabre neighbors. Kids even play soccer among the mausoleums.

The Bible teaches that there are only two classes of people, the living and the dead. That might be obvious, but according to the Word of God, not all of the living are truly alive and not all of the dead are truly dead. *"He who has the Son has life; he who does not have the Son of God does not have life" (1 John 5:12).*

David Douglas

Energetic Zeal

In 1825, Scottish botanist David Douglas sailed along the West Coast of the United States and up the Columbia River. At only 26 years old, the London native was on a quest to study the New World's plant life. Obsessed with plants since childhood, Douglas had been appointed to the Glasgow Botanical Gardens in Scotland.

As the ship approached land, one particular tree captivated David. As he reported, "So pleased was I that I could scarcely see [anything] but it." He couldn't wait to see the tree up close. When he did, he pronounced it "one of the most striking and truly graceful objects in nature." It was only fitting that this famous tree would later bear his name—the Douglas fir.

David spent the next two years exploring the Northwest, finding new plants and shipping more than 500 species back to England. William Hooker, one of the world's leading botanists, described David as a man of "great activity, undaunted courage, … and energetic zeal."

The Native Americans were immensely impressed with David's endurance, but they also questioned his sanity. They called him "Man of Grass" because he would hike from dawn to dusk collecting plants that he couldn't eat. There are more plants named for Douglas, more than 80, than for any other person in history.

On an 1829 trip, Douglas was collecting specimens in California and pulled a plant from the ground that had flecks of gold, which clung to its roots. But as David packed the plant for shipment, he saw only the plant. You see, Douglas had only one purpose in life. Nothing, not even gold, could distract him from his mission.

That is the same kind of focused, energetic zeal that God wants from us today! *"Fight the good fight of faith, lay hold on eternal life, to which you were also called and have confessed the good confession in the presence of many witnesses" (1 Timothy 6:12).*

Desmond Doss
A Man of Conscience

After being drafted, Desmond Doss' refusal to bear arms gave his commanders fits, and his fellow soldiers used the meek misfit as a punching bag. Ever resilient, he said that his faith forbade the taking of lives and promoted their saving. He always kept his Bible close by, but he refused to carry a weapon—even as self-defense.

Yet as an infantry medic during World War II, Doss did as much as any great warrior, if not more, to save the lives of his fellow men. During a bloody assault in Okinawa in April 1945, Doss exhibited magnificent fortitude in the face of extreme danger. He retrieved 75 wounded men off a rocky cliff while under constant enemy fire. Doss believed this impressive feat was made possible by the guiding hand of God. He received many wounds during that battle and others, but he always tended to the soldiers before taking care of himself.

His reputation as a soldier propelled his name as a symbol for gallantry above and beyond the call of duty. While seriously wounded after jumping on a grenade to protect his fellow men, Doss dragged himself through the battlefield to treat wounded soldiers until he was rescued. Doss later discovered he'd lost his Bible during the conflict. However, the respect of his fellow soldiers had grown so profound that they searched the battlefield until they found the beloved book of the private they had all once mocked.

For his heroic efforts and bravery, Doss received this country's highest honor. On Columbus Day in 1945, President Truman placed the Congressional Medal of Honor around Doss' neck and said, "This is a greater honor for me than being president." This made Doss the first conscientious objector to receive the award.

One day, those who are faithful to God will receive the greatest award of all because of the heroic efforts of Jesus. *"Finally, there is laid up for me the crown of righteousness, which the Lord, the righteous Judge, will give to me on that Day, and not to me only but also to all who have loved His appearing"* (2 Timothy 4:8).

Frank Hayes

Victory in Death

On June 4, 1923, jockey Frank Hayes, who had never won a race, took off through the gates at Belmont Park on Long Island. The horse he was riding that day was a twenty-to-one long shot called Sweet Kiss.

Incredibly, he and his outsider horse made it to the finish line first. But all was not well. Evidently, at some point during the race, Hayes had a heart attack and died, somehow staying in the saddle. Hayes' death was not even discovered until race officials came to congratulate him and his lifeless body dropped out of the saddle. Despite this, Frank and Sweet Kiss were declared the winners of the race.

Some speculated that the fatal heart attack may have been brought on by Hayes' extreme efforts to lose twelve pounds to qualify for the race. Others thought the shock that he was actually winning the race brought on the heart attack. The horse, Sweet Kiss, was nicknamed "Sweet Kiss of Death," and no jockey ever rode her in a race again.

Did you know that the Bible says the Christian life is a race that can be won only by dying first? *"For I am already being poured out as a drink offering, and the time of my departure is at hand. I have fought the good fight, I have finished the race, I have kept the faith"* (2 Timothy 4:6, 7).

George Washington Carver

A Humble Genius

Born to slave parents in Diamond Grove, Missouri, George Washington Carver was rescued from Confederate kidnappers as an infant. He began his education in southwest Missouri, where he worked as a farmhand and studied in a one-room schoolhouse. He is perhaps the nation's best-known African-American scientist and a man with an incredibly green thumb.

In the period between 1890 and 1910, when the cotton crop had been devastated by the boll weevil, Carver advised farmers to cultivate peanuts, and before long he developed more than 300 different peanut-based products—everything from milk to printer's ink.

At Tuskegee, Carver developed his crop rotation method, which alternated nitrate-producing legumes—such as peanuts and peas—with cotton, which depletes soil of its nutrients. Following Carver's lead, farmers in the south soon began planting peanuts one year and cotton the next.

While many of the peanuts were used to feed livestock, large surpluses quickly developed. When he discovered that the sweet potato and the peanut also enriched depleted soils, Carver found almost twenty additional uses for these crops, including making synthetic rubber and material for paving highways.

Throughout his life, Carver remained a humble man who attributed his success to his faith in Jesus. *"He who is of a proud heart stirs up strife, but he who trusts in the LORD will be prospered"* (Proverbs 28:25).

Gilberto Araujo

Walking into Your Own Funeral

In October 2012, Gilberto Araujo, a poor car washer from the streets of Sao Paulo, Brazil, had not seen his family in months. But nothing could prepare him for what he saw when he entered his mother's house, where scores of people had gathered. When they saw him, some fainted, some screamed, and others ran from the room in terror.

You see, in the middle of the room was an open coffin containing Gilberto's body. The family had come together to mourn his death, but it turned out to be a bizarre case of mistaken identity. Another car washer in the large Brazilian city, Genivaldo Santos Gama, had been murdered and happened to look exactly like Gilberto. When the police first found the body, they called Gilberto's family. The similarities were so striking that even his own brother identified the body as that of his younger sibling.

After recovering from the shock, the family was elated. Gilberto's mother Marina told reporters: "I am overjoyed. What mother wouldn't be after seeing her son is dead and then she sees him alive?"

The Bible tells us that resurrections have happened in the past and will happen again in the future! *"For the Lord Himself will descend from heaven with a shout, with the voice of an archangel, and with the trumpet of God. And the dead in Christ will rise first. Then we who are alive and remain shall be caught up together with them in the clouds to meet the Lord in the air. And thus we shall always be with the Lord"* (1 Thessalonians 4:16, 17).

Golden Gate Bridge

Safety First

When construction began on the Golden Gate Bridge—an incredible feat of engineering—in San Francisco on January 5, 1933, Joseph B. Strauss, the chief engineer, was adamant about using the most rigorous safety precautions in the history of bridge building.

He even commissioned a local manufacturer of safety equipment to design protective headgear that Strauss insisted workers wear on the job. This prototype of the modern hard hat was worn for the first time along with glare-free goggles. Special hand and face cream protected the workers against the constant biting wind, while special diets helped them fight dizziness.

The most conspicuous precaution was the safety net, suspended under the entire floor of the bridge from one end to the other. During construction, the net saved the lives of 19 men, who became known with affection as the "Half-Way-to-Hell Club."

Of course, the best safety net for Christians is to maintain a close relationship with Christ. *"I will both lie down in peace, and sleep; for You alone, O Lord, make me dwell in safety"* (Psalm 4:8).

Israel

An Extraordinary Nation

The state of Israel is one of the world's smallest countries—yet her people can make claim to many amazing accomplishments.

For instance, Israel's workforce has the highest ratio of university degrees to population in the world. And Israel's economy of $100 billion is larger than all of its immediate neighbors combined. It has the highest average standard of living in the Middle East and also exceeds the United Kingdom.

Moreover, Israel produces more scientific papers per capita than any other nation by a large margin—as well as one of the highest per capita rates of patents filed. It also lays claim to the world's second highest number of new books and home computers per capita. Israel is the only country in the world that entered this century with a net gain in its number of trees.

Israel also controls the second largest fleet of fighter aircraft and developed the airline industry's most impenetrable flight security. United States officials look to Israel for advice on how to handle external and internal security threats. Yet relative to its population, Israel is the largest immigrant-absorbing nation on earth.

It would certainly seem that God is blessing this little country! But why then is this unique nation so embattled? *"We looked for peace, but there was no good; and for the time of healing, and there was trouble" (Jeremiah 14:19).*

John Chapman

Legend of Johnny Appleseed

Most Americans have heard the legend of Johnny Appleseed, who travelled the frontier with a kettle on his head while scattering apple seeds. But unlike Pecos Bill and Paul Bunyan, there really was a Johnny Appleseed. His real name was John Chapman, and he lived between 1775 and 1845. John had an extraordinary love for apples, and he wanted everybody to be able to enjoy them. So he came down from Philadelphia with apple seeds he collected, and he planted them throughout the Ohio River Valley.

He roamed the countryside vigilantly looking for places young apple trees could flourish—usually by a spring or on the side of a hill with rich soil. With a prayer, he gently pushed the little seeds into the earth and then built a brush fence to protect the saplings before moving on to the next promising place.

Every fall, he'd return to the cider presses in Pennsylvania, where he selected good seeds from the discarded apple pressings. These he carefully washed, dried, and bagged for planting the following spring.

As the orchards grew, he would sell or trade the young trees to thousands of farmers who were settling the land. Even though he lived on the frontier, he didn't eat meat, but he always carried a stewpot or kettle with him. He has been pictured wearing a pot on his head, but more likely he kept it tied to the top of his backpack.

Chapman never married, but he was a religious man who loved people. As settlers moved into the wilderness, his lonely nights were fewer because he was a welcomed guest in every home. On most nights, he would hold settlers enthralled with his stories of the wild woods or read to them from the Bible he carried. As a result of practicing his favorite hobby for about fifty years, this one man provided mountains of apples to feed thousands of people for generations!

There is no way to estimate how many seeds Chapman planted or the number of orchards he created in the territory south of the

Great Lakes between the Ohio and Mississippi Rivers. Even to this day, that region is a rich source of beautiful apple trees.

Do you ever wonder what the world would be like if every Christian felt that same compelling desire to spread God's seeds of truth? *"He who sows sparingly will also reap sparingly, and he who sows bountifully will also reap bountifully" (2 Corinthians 9:6).*

Jerusalem's Underground Cemetery
Waiting for the Messiah

Throughout history, Jews from around the world have sought to have their remains laid to rest in Jerusalem. This has created a huge challenge for the city's sprawling cemeteries, which are unable to keep up with the demand. Since they can no longer spread out, and they can't go up, the only other option was to go down—in a big way.

Since 2014, a team of construction workers has been tunneling into stone under Jerusalem's largest cemetery to create a new vast underground burial site. When completed, it will contain about 23,000 graves in a series of interconnected hallways that span over half a mile. This massive underground beehive-like cemetery—with state-of-the-art lighting, elevators, and ventilation systems—will cost $57 million. Devout Jews believe the Scriptures teach that the Messiah will someday come to the Mount of Olives, so they want a resting place nearby for the resurrection day.

Did you know that the Bible teaches the Messiah has already made His first trip to the Mount of Olives? *"Now as He sat on the Mount of Olives, the disciples came to Him privately, saying, 'Tell us, when will these things be? And what will be the sign of Your coming, and of the end of the age?' "* (Matthew 24:3).

Kevin Coughlin

A Blind Man Sees

Doctors are mystified as to why a 55-year-old New York man, who was known to be blind for twenty years, suddenly began to see again. Kevin Coughlin, who has a hereditary condition called Leber Optic Neuropathy, awoke one day to discover his vision was miraculously returning without any medical treatment.

The spontaneous reversal of this disease, which destroyed his optic nerve cells, has never been documented before. The only thing Coughlin can think of is that he had begun to pray daily and eat more vegetables. Now he can actually lead his seeing-eye dog!

Did you know the Bible says that God is in the business of opening the eyes of the blind? *"To open blind eyes, to bring out prisoners from the prison, those who sit in darkness from the prison house" (Isaiah 42:7).*

Emma Morano
The Last Nineteenth Century Survivor

The world's oldest person and the last known to have been born in the 1800s died April 15, 2017. The Associated Press reported that Emma Morano of Italy, 117 years old, died tranquilly while sitting in a rocking chair in her home, located in the town of Verbania.

Morano was born on November 29, 1899, and her life spanned three centuries. She was believed to be the last-surviving person born in the nineteenth century. Morano was the oldest of eight children; her siblings and one child all preceded her in death, including a sister who lived to be 102. Morano worked in a twine factory and at a boarding school kitchen, retiring at age 75—more than 40 years ago.

When asked if she had any secrets for a long life, Emma explained that she ate simple food, did not overeat, and got plenty of rest. She went to bed early, sleeping at least ten hours every night. Her friends say she also had very good genetics. Indeed, doctors say the three most important things you can do to lengthen your life are to eat natural food, get plenty of exercise, and choose your ancestors carefully.

Did you know Scripture tells us that having the right family connections can actually lengthen your life? *"For whoever does the will of My Father in heaven is My brother and sister and mother"* (Matthew 12:50).

Leaning Tower of Pisa

Plan Carefully

The Leaning Tower of Pisa is a world-famous 183-foot bell tower in Pisa, Italy. Shortly after construction began in 1173, the builders noticed that it was not perfectly level. Because of the shallow foundation and silty soil, architects believed there was nothing they could do about the slight lean, so the project continued.

Despite a number of small wars and financial setbacks over the next two hundred years, the tower was eventually completed. In the centuries that followed, however, the tilt gradually increased until it was precariously 15 feet off vertical center.

By 1990, the iconic structure was at risk of toppling and was closed to the public. During the next decade, $40 million was spent to slightly straighten the leaning tower and reinforce the foundation, making it safe to reopen for tourists to visit the crooked monument.

Did you know the Bible says you need to lay your plans carefully before you build a tower or others will mock? *"Which of you, intending to build a tower, does not sit down first and count the cost, whether he has enough to finish it—lest, after he has laid the foundation, and is not able to finish, all who see it begin to mock him, saying, 'This man began to build and was not able to finish'?"* (Luke 14:28–30).

Alexander Selkirk

The Real Robinson Crusoe

Daniel Defoe's famous adventure novel *Robinson Crusoe* is the story of one man's courage and ability to survive the ultimate tests of nature. Yet few people know that Robinson Crusoe really did exist, but his real name was Alexander Selkirk. Defoe based his novel on Selkirk's real-life adventures.

Selkirk was born in 1676 in Fife, Scotland. This son of a tanner ran away in 1693 for the sea and eventually joined William Dampier on an expedition plundering Spanish merchant ships. In September 1704, after a serious quarrel with Captain Dampier, the hotheaded Selkirk requested that he be put ashore on the uninhabited island of Más a Tierra in the Juan Fernandez Archipelago, 400 miles west of Chile. (It was fortunate for Selkirk, because Dampier's ship later sank and most of the crew were lost.)

Selkirk's possessions included his clothes, bedding, a flintlock, gunpowder, bullets, a hatchet, a knife, a kettle, and a Bible. He built two huts from pimento trees, covered them with long grass, and lined them with the skins of goats, which were abundant on the island. He also made himself clothes with goat skins. When his gunpowder was spent, he created fire by rubbing two sticks together.

Great numbers of cats and rats plagued his island life. He eventually tamed many of the cats, and they would lie about by the hundreds but also deliver him from the rats. To entertain himself, he sang and danced. In time, he conquered the inconveniences of his solitude and found happiness on the island.

Selkirk remained alone on the island for more than four years. Finally, in February 1709, Captain Woodes Rogers discovered him while sailing the ship *Duke,* whose pilot happened to be old Captain Dampier. Despite his long castaway, Selkirk was given command of a captured Spanish ship. He returned to England in 1711, and his story was published. A few years later, Robinson Crusoe appeared.

Someone once said, "No man is an island." Although quiet time alone is a blessing, God never intended for us to live in isolation. *"The Lord God said, 'It is not good that man should be alone; I will make him a helper comparable to him' " (Genesis 2:18).*

Mihailo Tolotos

The Monk Who Never Saw a Woman

Mihailo Tolotos was likely the only healthy man in modern history who never saw the form or heard the voice of a woman. Mihailo, who became a monk, died in 1938 at the age of 82 in one of the monasteries atop Mount Athos in Greece.

So how did this come about? Well, after his mother passed away during his birth, Mihailo was taken to Athos. Not once in his life did he leave this monastic colony, which for more than 900 years has strictly excluded all females—both animal and human. Mihailo had only descriptions from others to visualize what a woman looks like.

Did you know that the Bible says our ability to visualize spiritual things is limited until Christ's return? *"For now we see in a mirror, dimly, but then face to face. Now I know in part, but then I shall know just as I also am known"* (1 Corinthians 13:12).

Chris Bertish

Paddleboarding the Atlantic

A 42-year-old South African surfer, Chris Bertish, accomplished what many thought was impossible. Bertish paddled a surfboard unassisted across the Atlantic Ocean. It took him 93 days to cover the 4,600 miles, and almost two million paddle strokes—all while standing up!

Photo credit: Allan Van Gysen

The epic journey took him from Morocco past the Canary Islands to English Harbour at Antigua in the Caribbean. His custom-built board was 20 feet in length and weighed 1,350 pounds. The board included a small cabin at the front end that allowed Bertish to take shelter from the elements—and a number of tech amenities such as a water maker, a satellite phone, a radio, a laptop, and a radar device to assist him on the journey.

Weather and exhaustion worked against him as he paddled 12 to 15 hours every day, surviving for nearly three months on freeze-dried meals. Because his board was riding low, his feet and ankles were almost constantly underwater. Waves threatened to swamp him, and he had several run-ins with sharks who tried to bite his surfboard to see if it was edible.

So why did Bertish endure this grueling three-month journey crossing an ocean on a surfboard? Well partly, it was to test the limits of paddleboard sports, but mostly it was to raise money for his favorite charities. He was able to raise $6 million through this historic journey.

Did you know that the Bible says charity is the noblest human motive? *"Charity suffereth long, and is kind; charity envieth not; charity vaunteth not itself, is not puffed up, doth not behave itself unseemly, seeketh not her own, is not easily provoked, thinketh no evil; rejoiceth not in iniquity, but rejoiceth in the truth; beareth all things, believeth all things, hopeth all things, endureth all things. Charity never faileth. ... And now abideth faith, hope, charity, these three; but the greatest of these is charity"* (1 Corinthians 13:4–8, 13 KJV).

The Moon

It's Not for Sale

In 1967, the United Nations adopted the international Outer Space Treaty, forbidding all nations from claiming the moon, or any part of space, as a territory. The treaty failed to mention anything about private individuals or corporations, however, leaving a rather large loophole.

In the early 1980s, Dennis Hope from Nevada sent letters to the United Nations, the United States, and the Soviet Union, informing them that he was claiming ownership of all planetary and lunar surfaces in our solar system—aside from the earth, of course. He even gave them the opportunity to respond if they had objections, but he never heard a word from them.

For nearly 40 years, Hope has been selling land plots on the moon, Mars, and other heavenly bodies for a reasonable price—about $20 an acre. And he's been pursuing this as not just a novelty sale, but as a serious real estate transaction, complete with covenants and bylaws that prevent the unsightly or trivial usage of the property. His sales are accelerating, and within a couple of years, he anticipates he'll have a constituency in the millions—enough to put serious pressure on the United Nations to recognize the government of Luna.

In the meantime, Hope continues to operate his company selling people "official" title to land on the moon. Although others are now in the same business, Hope has earned about $10 million since he began his out-of-this-world business. That averages out at $270,000 a year selling land on planets he has never been to and that he does not possess.

Did you know that the Bible teaches you can own heavenly real estate? And the price is already paid! *"In My Father's house are many mansions; if it were not so, I would have told you. I go to prepare a place for you. And if I go and prepare a place for you, I will come again and receive you to Myself; that where I am, there you may be also"* (John 14:2, 3).

Slavomir Rawicz

Pilgrimage to Freedom

In November 1939, young Polish lieutenant Slavomir Rawicz was arrested by the Russians following the German-Soviet invasion of Poland. Following 12 months of interrogation, he was sentenced to 25 years of hard labor for a bogus charge of spying. He was then sent off to Siberia.

With thousands of others, Rawicz was transported in open cattle trucks in sub-zero temperatures, to the end of the line at Irkutsk. At that point, the wretched prisoners were chained together and forced to march hundreds of miles to Camp 303, which the survivors had to then build for themselves from scratch.

In April 1941, with the aid of the camp commandant's wife, Rawicz and six others escaped in a blizzard. For the next year, they trekked 4,000 miles south through the Gobi Desert and over the Himalayas, on through Tibet until they reached India—where they were discovered by a Gurkha patrol.

Three of the seven died on the way. When rescued, Rawicz weighed only 70 pounds, but he went on to live to the age of 88. Through sheer determination and living off the land, he and three others had survived bitter cold, suffocating heat, thirst, starvation, and major injury in their epic quest for freedom.

Did you know that the message of the Bible is about a pilgrimage to freedom? *"These all died in faith, not having received the promises, but having seen them afar off were assured of them, embraced them and confessed that they were strangers and pilgrims on the earth. For those who say such things declare plainly that they seek a homeland. And truly if they had called to mind that country from which they had come out, they would have had opportunity to return. But now they desire a better, that is, a heavenly country. Therefore God is not ashamed to be called their God, for He has prepared a city for them"* (Hebrews 11:13–16).

Maewyn Succat
The Saint Behind the Legend

Typically on March 17, people all over the world celebrate Saint Patrick's Day. Cities like New York and Boston have large parades baptized in shamrocks, leprechauns, and green. Chicago even dyes its river green!

But there is far more myth than fact taught about this man of God. For starters, this patron saint of Ireland wasn't even Irish; he was Scottish. St. Patrick was born Maewyn Succat in Roman Britain around AD 389. He was captured by raiders when he was 16 and shipped to Ireland, where he was sold as a slave caring for pigs and sheep. While in captivity, he surrendered his heart to Christ.

After six years, he escaped back to his homeland. But later, he heard God call him to return to Ireland as a missionary to convert his captors. After he became a minister, he took on the name Patrick or Patricius, which means "father of the citizens."

Saint Patrick was not technically a saint because the Catholic Church never canonized him. Fantastic as it might seem, even though they built hundreds of churches that bear his name, Patrick was not even a Roman Catholic. He operated as an independent Christian and a self-supporting missionary. And finally, March 17th doesn't commemorate his birthday, but the day the old missionary is believed to have died in his beloved Ireland. During his 29 years as a missionary, Patrick baptized thousands of Irishmen and established at least 300 churches.

It's amazing how many fables have become connected with the work of this great missionary. But this is not the first time this has happened. For instance, the apostle Paul wrote of those who were spreading destructive fables about his evangelistic team. *"Why not say, 'Let us do evil that good may come'?—as we are slanderously reported and as some affirm that we say. Their condemnation is just" (Romans 3:8).*

The Vacationers
Bad Omens?

Jason and Jenny Cairns-Lawrence from the Midlands in England decided to spend their holiday in New York City. Unfortunately, their vacation happened to land on September 11, 2001, when the World Trade Center was attacked and nearly 3,000 people perished.

Rattled by their experience, they thought next they would vacation a little closer to home and went down to London. That was on July 7, 2005, and it turned into the day when four British suicide bombers attacked the London subway and the bus network. On that occasion, 52 people died and 700 people were injured.

For their holiday in 2008, Jason, a sales agent with a metal plating company, and Jenny, a dental laboratory worker, thought it might be more peaceful on the other side of the world, so they decided to vacation in Mumbai, India. You guessed it—the night of November 26 was when the city was attacked by terrorists and 180 people were killed. It seems that Jason and Jenny have a knack for being in the wrong place at the wrong time.

Have you ever wondered if some people are just naturally unlucky? Well, God has promised that those who are faithful to Him have no need to be concerned about their fate. *"We know that all things work together for good to those who love God, to those who are the called according to His purpose" (Romans 8:28).*

Ford's Fair Lane

The Big House

Henry Ford's mansion, named "Fair Lane," still stands in Dearborn, Michigan, filled with elaborately carved woodwork and technical wonders. For its location, Ford chose 1,300 beautiful acres overlooking the meandering River Rouge. His mansion features 56 rooms on three floors, covering 31,000 square feet. The price for constructing and furnishing it was about $2 million—and that was back in 1915, when a loaf of bread was a nickel.

Photo credit: Dave Parker

In addition to the main residence, the estate included a man-made lake, boat house, staff cottages, pony barn, skating house, greenhouse, extensive gardens, 350 varieties of roses, a working farm, agricultural research facilities, and 500 birdhouses.

Determined to be independent of public utilities, Ford built his own power plant, which was connected to the home by a 300-foot underground tunnel. The finely machined turbines fed electricity to the entire estate, providing light and power at the flick of a finger.

However, in April 1947, when torrential rains lashed down on the Detroit area, the River Rouge went on a rampage. It smothered the fire under the powerhouse boilers and caused the electricity to fail for the only time in 30 years. It happened to be the night Ford lay dying in his bedroom. Though surrounded by engineering marvels, he left the world as he had entered it 87 years earlier—in a cold house lit by candles, only two miles from the farm where he was born.

When Jesus died outside Jerusalem four miles from the place of His birth, the sky went dark and the veil in the temple was ripped from top to bottom. *"Now it was about the sixth hour, and there was darkness over all the earth until the ninth hour. Then the sun was darkened, and the veil of the temple was torn in two. And when Jesus had cried out with a loud voice, He said, 'Father, into Your hands I commit My spirit.' Having said this, He breathed His last"* (Luke 23:44–46).

Amou Haji
The Dirtiest Man in the World

Dermatologists tell us that bathing too often may not be good for your skin, but obviously, not bathing enough can cause serious social problems. Take, for example, Amou Haji, who has the distinction of being called the dirtiest man in the world.

Believing that washing would make him sick, Haji, who lives in the Fars province of Iran, has not had a shower or bath over the past sixty years. Haji, who is about 80 years old, says he chose this way of life after going through some emotional setbacks in his youth; since then, not surprisingly, he has become a bit isolated.

His clothing appears to be a collection of dirty rags and when he needs a haircut, he simply singes his hair with a burning stick. At night, he sleeps in a hole in the ground or in an open brick shack, which some concerned neighbors built for him. To relax, he likes to sit down and smoke a pipe packed with dung.

Once, a group of young men tried to give him a shower—but luckily, he says, he managed to escape. When asked if there is anything he wanted, he said he'd like to find a wife. Evidently, he has not yet figured out why he's having a problem with that.

Did you know that the Bible mentions a man who took seven baths in a single day? *"[Naaman] went down and dipped seven times in the Jordan, according to the saying of the man of God; and his flesh was restored like the flesh of a little child, and he was clean" (2 Kings 5:14).*

Leonardo da Vinci

Renaissance Man

It is nearly impossible to discuss the Renaissance without mentioning Leonardo da Vinci. Few have been born with an intellect that could match his genius. Da Vinci's artworks, like the Mona Lisa, are remarkable for their harmony, soft light, and sharpness of observation.

But Leonardo was more than just an artist; he was a genius in science, architecture, and engineering. His interests were so broad and numerous, it boggles the mind. He observed everything from the properties of herbs to the movements of the heavens. A century before Galileo, Leonardo was able to find new fundamental knowledge about time keeping and to connect it with machines, designing clocks that operated by weights, gears, and water.

In the fields of anatomy, botany, zoology, geology, hydrology, aerology, optics, and mechanics, he was far ahead of his time. He designed everything from fortifications, weapons, and engines of war to beautiful gardens, castles, churches, canals, and roads.

Leonardo loved animals and treated them with great kindness. Often, when passing a market where live birds were sold, he would let them out of their cages and pay the vendor the price. A vegetarian, Leonardo wrote, "I have from an early age renounced the use of meat, and the time will come when men such as I look upon the murder of animals as they now look upon the murder of men."

Many know Leonardo invented the scissors, but his other ideas were often far ahead of his time and only came to realization centuries after his death—such as the tank, the helicopter, and the parachute. In fact, in 2000, some Englishmen built a parachute according to Leonardo's specifications and tried it out: It worked perfectly!

Looking back on his drawings and designs, it almost seems as if Leonardo could see into the future. This naturally makes us wonder, can any man really know what's going to happen? Well, according to the Bible, only God truly knows the future. *"I am God, and there is none like Me, declaring the end from the beginning, and from ancient times things that are not yet done" (Isaiah 46:9, 10).*

Valley of Bones

A Picture of the Future

In 1942, a British forest guard was patrolling in the Himalayas, at about 16,000 feet, when he made a shocking discovery. There, at the bottom of a small valley, was a frozen lake full of human skeletons. During that warm summer, the melting of the ice revealed even more skeletal remains. Obviously, something horrible had happened there.

Was it war, landslide, avalanche, mass suicide, or plague? For years, no one knew. However, a 2004 expedition seems to have finally settled the mystery. Even though many of the bones still had flesh and hair, testing confirmed that all the skeletons were more than a thousand years old. The cold, dry climate had helped to preserve the remains.

All these people evidently died in a similar way, from blows to the head and shoulders—as if the blows had all come from above. Rings, spears, leather shoes, and bamboo staves were found, leading experts to believe that the group was comprised of pilgrims heading through the valley. DNA testing indicated that 70 percent of the victims had links to Iran; the remainder were ancestors of the local Indian population.

After much research, the 2004 expedition believed that all 300 people died in about AD 850 because they were caught unprotected by a sudden and severe hailstorm. This isn't hard to believe when you consider that 92 people were killed in Bangladesh in 1986 by a hailstorm dropping stones weighing up to a pound and a half.

Did you know that the Bible talks about a plague where perhaps hundreds of people were killed by giant hailstones? *"So there was hail, and fire mingled with the hail, so very heavy that there was none like it in all the land of Egypt since it became a nation. And the hail struck throughout the whole land of Egypt, all that was in the field, both man and beast; and the hail struck every herb of the field and broke every tree of the field"* (Exodus 9:24, 25).

Werner Forssmann

Fixer of the Human Heart

In Germany, a 25-year-old doctor, Werner Forssmann, had a radical idea. He proposed a new way to examine the human heart, but his idea was flatly rejected by hospital administrators. Forssmann's innovative idea was to send a thin catheter through a vein or artery directly into a living, pumping heart to have a better look around. It was revolutionary for 1929, and his superiors thought this kind of experiment would kill a patient. But Forssmann was convinced that by combining the catheter placement with an X-ray, physicians could detect heart problems much earlier and save lives.

Forssmann was determined to try this approach, so when his bosses said no, the young doctor decided to move forward anyway. He persuaded a young nurse to unlock the cabinet of catheters and to allow him to do the procedure on her. But while she was strapped to an operating table, he instead stuck the catheter into his own arm. She screamed for him to stop, but he went ahead. Then, with the help of the panicked nurse, Forssmann walked down a flight of stairs with the catheter in his heart and persuaded a reluctant technician to take an X-ray. He had made medical history! Then the hospital fired him.

Though marginalized by the medical community, Forssmann's bold experiments were studied by other scientists, who advanced his techniques. In 1956, Dr. Forssmann was working in another hospital when he received a phone call and was told that he had won the Nobel Prize for his innovative work on heart catheterization.

Yet even today with our incredible medical technology, nothing can see or repair the human heart in the way God can. This is why David prayed, "Search me, O God, and know my heart" (Psalm 139:23). *"For the Lord searches all hearts and understands all the intent of the thoughts" (1 Chronicles 28:9).*

AMAZING FACTS

Culture & History

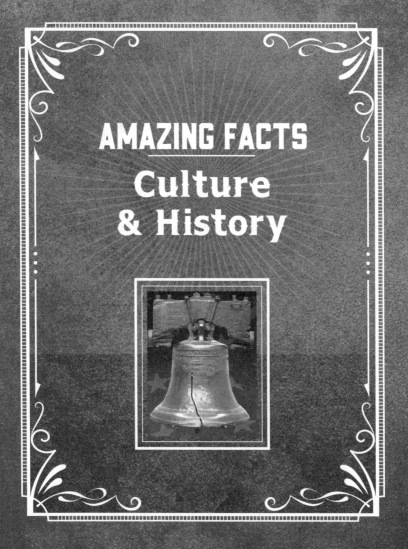

Church Attendance

Faith and Longevity

Religious services aren't just good for your soul—they can lengthen your life! A May 2016 study published by the American Medical Association says that those who frequently attend church services have a much better chance of living longer than those who don't.

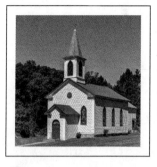

Over a 20-year span, the study surveyed a group of more than 76,000 female nurses. At the end of 20 years, more than 13,000 of them had died. But the study revealed that women who participated in religious services more than once a week were 33 percent less likely to be in the group who died, as compared to those who never attended services.

One of the team's most remarkable findings was on breast cancer. Women who attended services were no more or less likely to contract breast cancer, but those who attended church services were much more likely to survive.

Did you know that the Bible says only those who are in the house that's built on the rock will survive the storms of life? *"Let us consider one another in order to stir up love and good works, not forsaking the assembling of ourselves together, as is the manner of some, but exhorting one another, and so much the more as you see the Day approaching"* (Hebrews 10:24, 25).

Monopoly
WWII Edition

During World War II, the Nazis decided to allow Allied prisoners of war to have some board games to pass their endless months in confinement. Learning this, the British government conspired with the maker of the popular game Monopoly to smuggle into the prison camps escape kits that were cleverly hidden throughout the games.

For instance, within the stacks of Monopoly's fake money was real German and French currency. Silk maps of the German countryside were concealed within the box, and a compass and metal file were hidden inside the playing pieces. These clever kits helped several soldiers escape during the war.

Did you know that Jesus is in the business of helping prisoners escape from their bondage? *"The Spirit of the Lord GOD is upon Me, because the LORD has anointed Me to preach good tidings to the poor; He has sent Me to heal the brokenhearted, to proclaim liberty to the captives, and the opening of the prison to those who are bound" (Isaiah 61:1).*

American Television
A Vast Wasteland

In May 1961, Newton Minow, the then-chairman of the Federal Communications Commission, spoke to the National Association of Broadcasters on the topic of the "vast wasteland," saying, "I invite you to sit down in front of your television set when your station goes on the air and stay there without a book, magazine, newspaper, profit-and-loss sheet, or rating book to distract you—and keep your eyes glued to that set until the station signs off. I can assure you that you will observe a vast wasteland."

With that in mind, here are some interesting facts about television in America. Nearly 68 percent of teens have TV sets in their rooms. The average TV viewer has access to more than 200 channels. Watching TV is nearly a full-time job in most homes, with the average viewing time at 35 hours a week. The average American watches five hours a day; at this rate, that's nine years of TV if they live to be 75 years old!

Did you know the Bible emphasizes the importance of what we look at? *"Whatever things are true, whatever things are noble, whatever things are just, whatever things are pure, whatever things are lovely, whatever things are of good report, if there is any virtue and if there is anything praiseworthy—meditate on these things"* (Philippians 4:8).

The 28-Hour Sermon

Biblically Long-winded

A 46-year-old Anglican vicar from Lancashire, England, delivered a 28-hour, 45-minute sermon to establish a world record for the longest unscripted speech. Chris Sterry began this marathon sermon on June 29, 2001. While speaking, the former Old Testament professor was not allowed to repeat himself, talk nonsense, or pause for more than ten seconds—though he was permitted a 15-minute break every eight hours.

Sterry's sermon covered the first four books of the Bible and was broadcast live every 15 minutes on CNN throughout June 30. He undertook the challenge as a way of raising money for his church. His biggest wish? "I hope that those who come to listen to it will get something out of it." News reports do not indicate whether any of his parishioners went the distance with him.

Did you know that the Bible refers to the faith-generating value of a Spirit-filled sermon? *"So then faith comes by hearing, and hearing by the word of God"* *(Romans 10:17)*.

Alcohol and Lincoln
A Legend of Tragedy

Legend has it that two fatal drinks changed history. On the last day of Lincoln's life, the great emancipator said: "We have cleared up a colossal job. Slavery is abolished. After reconstruction, the next great question will be the overthrow and suppression of the legalized liquor traffic."

That evening, John Wilkes Booth stepped into a saloon to fill himself with liquor to nerve himself for his evil plan. That same night, Lincoln's bodyguard left the theater for a drink of liquor at that same saloon. While he was away, Booth shot Lincoln. These two drinks were among the costliest in American history.

Did you know God's Word strongly warns of the troubles brought on by consuming alcoholic beverages? *"Wine is a mocker, strong drink is a brawler, and whoever is led astray by it is not wise"* (Proverbs 20:1).

Comet Crash
Cracks from Stress

On January 10, 1954, a British-built de Havilland Comet, one of the first commercial jet airliners, tore apart in mid-air and crashed into the Mediterranean Sea, killing all 35 passengers and crew. Then two other Comets mysteriously went down in similar disasters.

Engineers eventually discovered that the square windows were the fatal design error. Stresses and fatigue were concentrated around the sharp corner points of the windows, and over time, the plane fuselage cracked, causing a catastrophic loss of pressure. This is why all commercial airliners today have rounded windows.

The Bible says that too much stress and fatigue can also make people crack and fall apart. Stress is linked to the six leading causes of death in the United States: heart disease, cancer, lung ailments, accidents, cirrhosis of the liver, and suicide. But God has a much better plan for our lives. *"Come to Me, all you who labor and are heavy laden, and I will give you rest" (Matthew 11:28).*

St. Francis Dam Break

Without Warning

At midnight on March 12, 1928, one of the worst catastrophes in California history occurred—the St. Francis Dam broke. Huge torrents of water washed down the San Francisquito Canyon, killing hundreds in its path. The official body count was 431 dead, but the actual number was substantially higher, since San Francisquito Canyon was home to hundreds of transient farm workers who

were never counted. This would bring the death toll to higher than that caused by the famous 1906 San Francisco earthquake.

The dam broke just under two years after its completion. More than 900 buildings and $7 million in property were destroyed in the flood. But the greatest tragedy of this disaster was that no one needed to perish!

There was ample warning time on the morning it broke. A worker at the dam saw water leaking through the dam wall. He warned his boss, William Mulholland, about this danger. After looking at the dam, Mulholland, who also designed the structure, decided that there was no cause for concern. But that night the dam broke, sending a wall of water as high as 140 feet down the canyon through Saugus, Fillmore, Santa Paula, and finally into the Pacific Ocean. It traveled 54 miles in 5.5 hours, destroying everything in its path.

The wall of standards separating the church from the world has more than a little seepage; indeed, a major breach is about to hemorrhage. *"Do you not know that friendship with the world is enmity with God? Whoever therefore wants to be a friend of the world makes himself an enemy of God"* (James 4:4).

A Debt-Free America

Yes. It Really Happened

In 1829, when President Andrew Jackson took office, the United States debt was around $58 million. In his inaugural address, he expressed his concern for the country's financial woes by saying, "It would appear that advantage must result from the observance of a strict and faithful economy. This I shall aim … [to] facilitate the extinguishment of the national  debt, the unnecessary duration of which is incompatible with real independence, and because it will counteract that tendency to public and private profligacy."

Jackson carried through on his promise and eventually erased all of Washington's red ink by paying off the national debt in full in 1835. Today, the nation's debt has risen to more than $10 trillion!

The Bible tells us that we are made debt free and reconciled to God through the precious blood of Jesus. *"For you were bought at a price; therefore glorify God in your body and in your spirit, which are God's" (1 Corinthians 6:20).*

Enigma Machines
How to End a World War

During World War II, the German army effectively used modified Enigma machines to communicate details of planned attacks on the Allies. Enigma machines relied on complex encrypted codes to make it nearly impossible for anyone without the codes to crack a message, even with another Enigma machine!

But in 1941, the British destroyer *HMS Bulldog* captured a German U-boat that had not only an Enigma, but also all the needed codes that were being used by the Nazis. It is believed that this event shortened the war by many years and saved thousands of lives.

Scripture says that only through God's Spirit can we understand the messages He has given us in His Word. *"Now we have received, not the spirit of the world, but the Spirit who is from God, that we might know the things that have been freely given to us by God. … But the natural man does not receive the things of the Spirit of God, for they are foolishness to him; nor can he know them, because they are spiritually discerned"* (1 Corinthians 2:12, 14).

The World's Longest Flight
Still Nothing Compared to Nature

The world's longest commercial airline flight is from Dubai, United Arab Emirates, to Auckland, New Zealand, covering more than 8,800 miles and lasting about 17 hours. That's a really long trip—especially if you have the middle seat. Yet that is nothing compared to how long some birds can stay aloft.

Thanks to the development of miniature lightweight electronic tags, researchers have discovered that the common swift is able to fly for ten months straight! Scientists in Sweden carefully monitored the movements of 13 swifts over the course of two years. They noted three of the birds did not land even once for ten months. Now that's a long flight! Swifts can travel millions of miles during their lifetimes, which average about five-and-a-half years, migrating between Europe and Africa with the seasons.

These energetic birds pluck insects from the air as they fly, but how do they sleep? Evidently, each day at dusk and dawn, the swift flies up to an altitude of about two miles. From there it is assumed the birds take catnaps while gliding down—but no one's really sure.

How would you like to be able to fly or run without ever feeling fatigue? The Bible says that one day this will be possible for God's people. *"But those who wait on the LORD shall renew their strength; they shall mount up with wings like eagles, they shall run and not be weary, they shall walk and not faint"* (Isaiah 40:31).

Gutenberg Bibles

A Priceless Treasure

Photo credit: Joshua Keller

Johannes Gutenberg's printing press has been called the most important invention of the last one thousand years. For approximately 4,500 years before the printing press came into existence, books were produced meticulously by hand, written on surfaces of clay, papyrus, wax, and parchment.

Back then, only the wealthy could afford books. But with the introduction of Gutenberg's press in the1450s, the production of books was revolutionized. Within sixty years, printing presses in operation throughout Western Europe produced more than twenty million books.

The Gutenberg Bible was the first major book printed, with 200 copies produced. Amazingly, 49 of them still exist today and are considered the most valuable books in the world. Each one is worth more than $35 million.

How ironic to consider that most of these priceless Bibles are never read as they sit in private vaults and lonely museums. The precious, life-giving truths they contain are what make them truly priceless. *"Your word I have hidden in my heart, that I might not sin against You" (Psalm 119:11).*

Identity Theft
Broken and Ruined Lives

Identity theft is a rampant crime in America. It happens when someone wrongfully obtains and uses another individual's personal data for fraud or deception, typically for economic gain. Unlike your fingerprints, your personal data—especially your Social Security number, bank account or credit card number, or telephone calling card PIN—can be terribly abused if they fall into the wrong hands, profiting others at your expense.

Every day, thousands of people across the country report funds stolen from their accounts. And each year, more than $16 billion is lost to identity thieves. In the worst cases, criminals completely take over victims' identities, run up vast debts and commit crimes, leaving the victims with destroyed credit and a criminal record that can take years to correct.

Did you know that the devil tried to steal your identity, leaving you in debt and with a criminal record beyond your means to repay? He leaves us with broken and ruined lives, and the Bible says that how we think about ourselves has a great impact on how we behave: *"For as he thinks in his heart, so is he"* (Proverbs 23:7). But there's hope in Jesus who ransomed our hijacked lives! *"You were ransomed from the futile ways inherited from your forefathers, not with perishable things such as silver or gold, but with the precious blood of Christ, like that of a lamb without blemish or spot"* (1 Peter 1:18, 19, ESV).

Krakatoa Eruption
Sonic Blast

One of the loudest sounds in world history was the volcanic explosion of Krakatoa in Indonesia in 1883. The blast's power was equivalent to about 200 megatons of dynamite and could be heard more than 3,000 miles away! More than 36,000 people were killed, and 165 coastal villages were destroyed—mostly by the giant sea waves that reached heights of 120 feet.

The deadly waves devastated everything in their path, hurling ashore coral blocks that weighed as much as 600 tons, while traveling a distance of 3,800 nautical miles in 12 hours. The tremendous explosion blew debris 15 miles into the atmosphere, which settled over an area of 300,000 square miles.

The massive dust cloud blocked out sunlight, plunging Jakarta, 100 miles away, into eerie darkness. For more than three months, the residual dust and smoke produced some of the most beautiful, unusual, and brilliant-red sunsets the world has witnessed. Three months after the eruption, the vivid flaming sunsets were so intense that fire engines were summoned in New York to quench imaginary infernos.

Moreover, fine ash 50 miles up in the stratosphere circled the equator. The volcanic dust veil created such spectacular atmospheric effects as blue and green moons and also acted as a solar radiation filter, lowering global temperatures as much as two degrees. Temperatures did not return to normal for five years.

The eruption of Krakatoa was one of the loudest, most powerful and visible events in modern times. Did you know that the book of Revelation pictures brilliant and powerful angels in the heavens proclaiming a loud message of warning and hope just prior to Jesus' return? *"And I looked, and I heard an angel flying through the midst of heaven, saying with a loud voice, 'Woe, woe, woe to the inhabitants of the earth, because of the remaining blasts of tho trumpet of the three angels who are about to sound!' "* (Revelation 8:13).

World's Largest Building

The Boeing Factory

By volume, the world's largest building is the Boeing Factory in Everett, Washington. This is where the company assembles the wide-body 747, 767, 777, and the 787 Dreamliner aircraft. The massive building covers nearly a hundred acres and contains more than 472 million cubic feet. It is so big you could fit all of Disneyland inside and still have room left over.

Photo credit: Maurice King

The Everett Boeing Factory also employs more than 30,000 people and includes its own fire department, security team, daycare center, and fitness center.

Did you know the Bible talks about a dwelling place that is even bigger? *"Heaven is My throne, and earth is My footstool. Where is the house that you will build Me? And where is the place of My rest?"* (Isaiah 66:1).

The Liberty Bell

Let Freedom Ring

The Liberty Bell, sometimes called Old Independence, is an enduring symbol of American patriotism, but it had a rough beginning.

Originally cast in London in 1752 and weighing more than two thousand pounds, the bell arrived in Philadelphia in September but cracked during its first test ringing. It was then melted down in Philadelphia and recast to make a second bell in June 1753. Unfortunately, this new bell was deemed to have poor tone, so it was melted down again and recast.

This is the celebrated Liberty Bell that exists today, which is made mostly of copper and tin with small amounts of lead, zinc, arsenic, gold, and silver. It hangs from what is believed to be its original yoke, made from 200 pounds of American elm. When struck, the bell sounds the note of E flat.

During the Revolutionary War, the bell was placed on a wagon, moved 60 miles west to Allentown, and hidden in the floorboards of the Zion Reformed Church—all in an effort to keep it from falling into British hands, who would have likely melted it down to make cannons.

After the war, it was rung every July 4 until sometime around 1835, when it cracked again. No one knows exactly when the Liberty Bell cracked the second time. Today, the 250-year-old icon is a popular attraction in Philadelphia and continues to be an icon of liberty.

Did you know that the bell gained its popularity as the "Liberty Bell," not by patriots of the Revolution, but by the abolitionists fighting against slavery? They chose this name because of the Bible inscription on the bell from Leviticus 25:10, which reads, "Proclaim liberty throughout all the land to all its inhabitants." It was a remarkably apt metaphor for a country that was literally split over slavery.

Jesus said that whoever commits sin is a slave of sin. So how much does real liberty cost? *"You were not redeemed with corruptible things, like silver or gold, from your aimless conduct received by tradition from your fathers, but with the precious blood of Christ" (1 Peter 1:18, 19).*

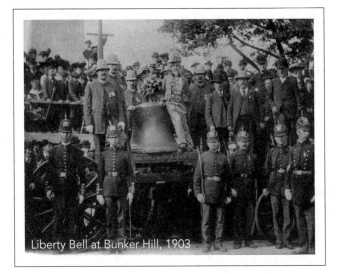

Liberty Bell at Bunker Hill, 1903

Military Superpower

Armageddon at the Door

For about five hundred years, the Roman Empire was the undisputed military powerhouse. It conquered most of the Western world—a feat made possible by their heavy investment in military war machines.

With 195 countries in the world today, the United States spends the most for its armed forces—taking up 42 percent of the world's military expenditures. In other words, almost half of the world's military investment is made by one country! Indeed, just in 2016, the United States spent $611 billion on the military, whereas China, the country in second place, spent $215 billion. No wonder the United States remains, by far, the most powerfully armed nation on earth—and the "world's only military superpower."

General Douglas MacArthur, warning of the perils of war in the age of nuclear weapons, said after the end of World War II, "We have had our last chance. If we will not devise some greater and more equitable system, Armageddon will be at our door." The book of Revelation, chapter 13, identifies two beasts in the last days that will try to compel worship. It will certainly require a large military power to enforce such a rule.

Did you know that the Bible also foretells that an escalation of war will be one of the signs of the last days? *"You will hear of wars and rumors of wars. See that you are not troubled; for all these things must come to pass, but the end is not yet. For nation will rise against nation, and kingdom against kingdom. And there will be famines, pestilences, and earthquakes in various places"* (Matthew 24:6, 7).

Tornado in D.C.

Liberty Whirlwind

In August 1814, America nearly lost its independence from Great Britain. The British army had successfully broken through national defensive lines and set fire to U.S. federal buildings all across Washington, D.C. This was the only time since the American Revolutionary War that a foreign power captured and occupied the U.S. capital.

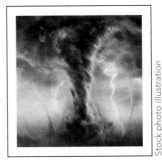

Stock photo illustration

Morale among the American soldiers was devastated, and they seemed to have lost their will to fight. It looked as though the United States was about to fall back into the hands of the British Empire.

Then suddenly dark clouds gathered, bringing a freak storm and the first-ever recorded tornado in the city's history. Along with a torrential downpour of rain, the twister rampaged through the capital. The whirlwind decimated the British army, damaged their ships, and at the same time, put out most of the fires they had set—totally changing the course of the war and helping to save the fledgling nation. As a result, the British occupation of Washington, D.C., lasted only about 26 hours.

Did you know that the Bible says God used wild weather to deliver a nation? *"And it happened, as they fled before Israel and were on the descent of Beth Horon, that the LORD cast down large hailstones from heaven on them as far as Azekah, and they died. There were more who died from the hailstones than the children of Israel killed with the sword" (Joshua 10:11).*

Traffic Signals

The Story of a Life Saver

Until the end of the nineteenth century, traffic in large cities was mostly uncontrolled chaos. Carriages, wagons, and horses dashed about in every direction, and getting across a busy street could be a life-and-death situation. In the 1860s, the NYPD formed the "Broadway Squad," whose primary duty was to escort pedestrians safely across the bedlam of Broadway!

In the 1890s, the traffic pandemonium in New York increased with the bicycle craze. This inspired Police Commissioner Theodore Roosevelt to organize a police bicycle squad—nicknamed the "Scorcher Squad"—to control speed demons who were constantly breaking the 8-mph speed limit.

Then with the advent of automobiles, it became even more of a challenge to negotiate the thunderous maze of travelers on streets that were often unpaved, muddy, or dusty! The early cars frequently broke down, clogging busy streets more than ever, and it was not uncommon to see traffic disputes settled by fist fights. It soon became apparent that some method of regulating traffic was a necessity.

Most cities had police directing traffic, which was among the most dangerous assignments. Scores of police officers were injured and killed; many died from constant exposure to weather extremes and the daily breathing in of the brew of dust, manure, and auto exhaust. Some cities tried a confusing system of train signals to regulate traffic. London even had gas-powered lamps, but they often blew up.

Then in 1912, Lester Wire, a detective on the Salt Lake City police force, thought of the words of Jesus in Matthew 5:15: "Nor do they light a lamp and put it under a basket, but on a lampstand, and it gives light to all who are in the house." This inspired him to invent one of the world's first electric traffic signals: a wooden box with red and green colored lights, up on a pole where cars could see it. Soon the idea spread to other cities, where it was improved and refined. Think of how many lives have been saved by the simple application of Scripture! *"The entrance of Your words gives light; it gives understanding to the simple" (Psalm 119:130).*

The Wicked Bible

An Innocent Mistake?

You already know that the first book ever mass produced on a printing press was the Bible. But the quality and methods of printing in those days were primitive, leading to many printing errors in these early Bibles. Although most didn't cause any serious theological confusion, some of them were still worth a smile.

That is, until 1631—when King Charles I ordered a reprint of the King James Bible from an English printer named Robert Barker. Only after the Bibles were delivered did anyone notice this serious mistake: In Exodus 20:14, a very small word was forgotten by the printers—"not." That might seem like a small mistake in a book with more than 700,000 words. But Exodus 20:14 happens to be one of the Ten Commandments. This little error changed the seventh commandment to say: "Thou shalt commit adultery"! As a result, this legendary edition became known as the "Wicked Bible."

King Charles was not amused by the infamous printing blunder. He ordered the Bibles recalled and destroyed, took away Barker's license to print Bibles, and fined him 300 pounds—a lifetime of wages in those days. Only 10 of the original 1,000 Wicked Bibles are in existence today.

Robert Barker's mistake was an innocent one, but the Bible tells us that the Beast power will deliberately try to change God's law. *"He shall speak pompous words against the Most High, shall persecute the saints of the Most High, and shall intend to change times and law" (Daniel 7:25).*

World's Worst Traffic Jam

A Five-Day Nightmare

According to a Texas A&M University study, the average American spends about 38 hours a week stuck in traffic. That means over the course of their working career, a person might spend up to three months creeping along in gridlock.

Stock photo illustration

But some countries have it even worse. On August 14, 2010, Chinese commuters experienced the worst traffic jam in history. Major road construction combined with massive trucking shipments locked up 60 miles of the China National Highway 110 for more than a week. Many drivers were only able to move their vehicles half a mile per day, and some drivers reported being stuck in the massive traffic jam for five days. This became an economic boom for local vendors, who sold stranded motorists food and water at greatly inflated prices.

Did you know that the Bible talks about one major highway that is never congested? *"Enter by the narrow gate; for wide is the gate and broad is the way that leads to destruction, and there are many who go in by it. Because narrow is the gate and difficult is the way which leads to life, and there are few who find it"* (Matthew 7:13, 14).

AMAZING FACTS

Science & Technology

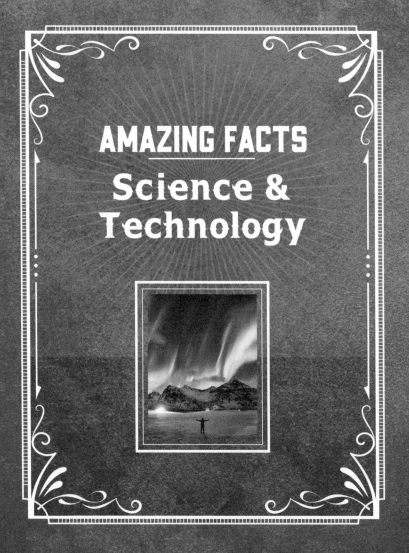

A 10,000-Year Clock

Annual Tick Tock

To demonstrate the importance of thinking ahead, Amazon.com founder and billionaire Jeff Bezos has dedicated $42 million to building a clock. But not just any clock! The 10,000-Year Clock is designed to measure time on a millennial scale.

Stock photo illustration

The clock's creator, Danny Hillis, has a vision for a timepiece that ticks once every year, with a century hand that moves just once every 100 years and a cuckoo that emerges every 1,000 years. The clock is now under construction on property owned by Bezos in a remote Texas desert. A 500-foot-deep tunnel will house the mechanism.

According to the Long Now Foundation that oversees the project, the clock will be powered by capturing energy from changes in temperature. The clock's chime generator will also create a different bell-ringing sequence each day for 10,000 years. Carved into the mountain adjacent to the clock are five room-sized anniversary chambers for the 1-year, 10-year, 100-year, 1,000-year, and 10,000-year anniversaries. In the first room, the clock will activate and run a planetary model once a year.

According to the clock's website, visitors will be welcome to view the massive timepiece, but you should be prepared for a rough trip. The nearest airport is several hours away by car and you must scale a rugged two-thousand feet by trail to reach the clock.

Did you know the Bible says that God is going to give the devil a thousand-year timeout after Jesus returns to earth? *"He laid hold of the dragon, that serpent of old, who is the Devil and Satan, and bound him for a thousand years; and he cast him into the bottomless pit, and shut him up, and set a seal on him, so that he should deceive the nations no more till the thousand years were finished"* (Revelation 20:2, 3).

Aluminum

A Common Precious Metal

It is used in everything from soda cans to aircraft to smartphones. It's light, strong, corrosion-resistant, non-magnetic, non-toxic, and naturally good looking. We are talking about aluminum. But if you live outside the United States, you call it "aluminium." This is because the British didn't think the elemental word aluminum was flashy enough for such a precious metal, so they added an extra vowel.

You see, shortly after aluminum was first discovered in the early nineteenth century, because it was so difficult to obtain, it was considered among the most precious metals on earth. At that time, it was worth more by weight than gold or platinum. Indeed, because it was so precious in 1884, the U.S. government commissioned a nine-inch pyramid of the metal to use as the apex of the Washington Monument. At that time, at 6.2 pounds, it was the largest single piece of solid aluminum ever cast. Soon after this, researchers found a new method to extract aluminum from common bauxite and the price of the metal plunged. In fact, scientists now know that aluminum is among the earth's most abundant minerals, making up 8 percent of the world's land mass.

Perhaps it shouldn't surprise us, then, that the Bible says gold, which is so precious in this world, will be as common as asphalt in the new earth. *"The twelve gates were twelve pearls: each individual gate was of one pearl. And the street of the city was pure gold, like transparent glass" (Revelation 21:21).*

Water Treatment

Life-Saving Liquid

Did you know that about three out of four Americans are chronically dehydrated? That's a problem when you consider that even just mild dehydration will slow down metabolism as much as 3 percent. Indeed, a lack of water is the number-one trigger of daytime fatigue.

Some research indicates that 8 to 10 glasses of water a day could also significantly ease back and joint pain. Drinking 16 ounces of water was shown to increase metabolism by 24 to 30 percent for up to 1.5 hours. And a mere two percent drop in body water can trigger fuzzy short-term memory, trouble with basic math, and difficulty focusing on the computer screen or on a printed page. Drinking five glasses of water daily significantly reduces the risk of colon cancer and bladder cancer by 49 percent.

It's obvious that a sufficient amount of water can eliminate or ease a whole host of common health problems. The Bible also teaches that Living Water can do the same for spiritual dehydration! *"On the last day, that great day of the feast, Jesus stood and cried out, saying, 'If anyone thirsts, let him come to Me and drink. He who believes in Me, as the Scripture has said, out of his heart will flow rivers of living water' " (John 7:37, 38).*

Liquid Paper

Hiding Your Mistakes

In the 1950s, Bette Nesmith had a good secretarial job at a Dallas bank. This was where she noticed a problem that kept intriguing her. Before the days of digital word processors, correcting a typing error was a difficult and messy process. She thought there must be a better way. Having had some art experience, she knew that artists often painted over their errors. At home, Bette put some white, water-based paint in a little bottle and with a small paint brush she took her simple invention to the office.

It worked perfectly. So, for five years, Bette quietly used her white correction paint to cover typing mistakes. Even though some bosses frowned on the practice, soon all the secretaries in her building were using what she called "Mistake Out."

With help from her son's high school chemistry teacher, she improved the formula to dry more quickly. Her invention was so popular that Bette attempted to sell the product idea to various companies, but they all turned her down.

In 1956, Bette began selling her typewriter correction fluid out of her kitchen, later expanding to a portable building in her backyard. As the product became an indispensable tool of the secretarial trade, she formed her own company and changed the product name to Liquid Paper. By 1979, her company was thriving—employing 200 people and making 25 million bottles of Liquid Paper annually. The Gillette Company eventually bought Bette's company for $47.5 million. It turns out that a simple invention to cover mistakes was a very popular idea!

Don't you wish there was an invention that would cover the mistakes of life? " 'Come now, and let us reason together,' says the LORD, 'Though your sins are like scarlet, they shall be as white as snow' " (Isaiah 1:18).

Nuclear Submarines

Sea Boomers

Nuclear submarines, or "Boomers," are among the most sophisticated engineering wonders in the world. They are equivalent to a tightly packed, self-contained city where a crew of about 140 shares the same space for up to six months.

The nuclear reactor provides heat energy, which is converted to electricity. This power is used to turn the propeller and send the submarine through the water. Because they carry their energy source with them, nuclear submarines are able to travel indefinitely. Their only limitation is food supply.

Boomers are deployed for months and can stay submerged for as long as ninety days. The crew has little contact with family during this time; combined with the pressure of being prepared to launch nuclear weapons, this makes it one of the most stressful assignments in the military. To compensate, the Navy trains the best chefs for these subs. A meal might consist of prime rib, lobster tails, sautéed mushrooms, baked potatoes, fresh bread, and real chocolate cake for dessert. And all this is done in an 8-by-10-foot galley that is barely larger than the kitchen in a small apartment. You can understand why submariners are the only fighting force that gains weight during deployment. Indeed, many of these submarine chefs, upon leaving the service, are hired by prestigious restaurants, cruise ships, and even the White House.

They say an army travels on its stomach. So why do many Christians believe that God does not care what His soldiers eat? He does. *"Why do you spend money for what is not bread, and your wages for what does not satisfy? Listen carefully to Me, and eat what is good, and let your soul delight itself in abundance"* (Isaiah 55:2).

Chelyabinsk Meteor
The Superbolide

On the morning of February 15, 2013, the Chelyabinsk meteor surprised everyone when it shot across the sky over Russia, exploding 18 miles above the earth in a blast of light 30 times brighter than the sun. The 65-foot-wide rock—roughly the size of a five-bedroom home—weighed 14,000 tons, making it heavier than the Eiffel Tower.

Photo credit: Aleksandr Ivanov

It is estimated that the meteor was traveling at 42,000 miles per hour when it entered the atmosphere, producing an explosion with kinetic energy about thirty times stronger than the atomic bomb that struck Hiroshima. About 1,500 people were treated for injuries, mostly from flying glass caused by the shockwave, which blew out windows in the area. The flash from the "superbolide" was so bright, many nearby observers were sunburned by its radiance. Strangely, even though hundreds of astronomers around the world are constantly scanning the heavens searching for potentially dangerous asteroids and meteors, nobody saw this one coming.

The Bible says that the second coming of Jesus will be brighter, louder, and more surprising than any random meteor. *"For as the lightning comes from the east and flashes to the west, so also will the coming of the Son of man be"* (Matthew 24:27).

The Doldrums

Dreary Eerie

Nothing was so feared by sailors in the days when ocean vessels were driven by wind than the doldrums. The doldrums are a part of the ocean near the equator that abound with prolonged calms and light, baffling winds.

The old sailing vessels, when caught in doldrums, would sometimes lie helpless for days or even weeks, waiting for the wind to begin blowing. There the weather is hot, humid, and extremely dispiriting; sometimes driving the irritable sailors to violence or insanity. Surprisingly, most hurricanes and severe squalls also originate within the doldrums.

Though it often seems we are at the mercy of weather conditions, there is One whose power exceeds any storm on land or sea. *"For He commands and raises the stormy wind, which lifts up the waves of the sea" (Psalm 107:25). "Then He arose and rebuked the wind, and said to the sea, 'Peace, be still!' And the wind ceased and there was a great calm" (Mark 4:39).*

Quiet Zone
The Green Bank Telescope

It may be hard to imagine, but there is a town three hours west of Washington, D.C., where cell phones, radio, television, Wi-Fi, and Bluetooth are forbidden. Green Bank, West Virginia, population 143, is home to the world's largest steerable radio telescope—the Robert C. Byrd Green Bank Telescope (GBT). The telescope is taller than the Statue of Liberty, and the

dish surface area is large enough to fit a college football stadium. This is why locals say GBT actually stands for "Great Big Thing."

The GBT is a highly sophisticated device that is extremely sensitive to even the faintest radio pulses traveling from distant galaxies. For the same reason, the telescope is also extremely susceptible to local electronic interference. The restrictions were introduced in the 1950s, when the Federal Communications Commission created the National Radio Quiet Zone—a 13,000-square-mile section of West Virginia where the Allegheny Mountains help create a natural barrier from radio transmissions.

The instruments in the GBT are so sensitive, they would be able to detect a transistor radio on Mars. Any device in the quiet zone that generates electromagnetic radiation—even a garage door opener—can distort its readings. And so the people who live in these parts must, by law, forego some of the gadgets that most of us take for granted. But they don't seem to mind. It's hard to miss the irony that scientists in the Radio Quiet Zone are using some of the world's most advanced instruments, but they can't heat their lunch with a microwave.

Did you know that the Bible says we all need a quiet zone? *"Be still, and know that I am God"* (Psalm 46:10).

Human Speed
World's Fastest People

The world record for the fastest a human has ever run is held by Usain Bolt, who was clocked at nearly 28 miles per hour in the 100-meter sprint. The current land speed record stands at 763 mph, set in October 1997 by British Royal Air Force pilot Andy Green, driving the jet-powered "Thrust SSC" (Super Sonic Car) in Nevada's Black Rock Desert.

The fastest that humans have ever flown was achieved by the crew of NASA's Apollo 10 moon mission—Thomas Stafford, John W. Young, and Eugene Cernan—as they rocketed back to our planet from the moon on May 26, 1969. They reached a top speed of 24,791 mph. That's approximately 32 times the speed of sound. That 46-year-old record still remains today as the fastest that any human beings have ever traveled.

But did you know the Bible speaks of individuals who apparently traveled even faster? *"Then they willingly received Him into the boat, and immediately the boat was at the land where they were going" (John 6:21).*

Aurora Borealis

Colors of Heaven

No words are adequate to describe the magnificent splendor of the Aurora Borealis. This spectacular natural display, also called the Northern or Southern Lights, are seen predominantly around the polar regions.

The luminous marvel can appear in colors of red, green, yellow, blue, and violet—as well as a variety of forms, like patches of light, streamers, arcs, rays, or even shimmering draperies. The Northern Lights have been described since ancient times, but only recently has humanity discovered the cause of this phenomenon. The sun gives off high-energy charged particles, or ions, that speed through space at more than one million miles per second. When this stream of plasma, or solar wind, strikes the earth's magnetic field, it is channeled toward the polar regions. When these electrically charged particles collide with the gases in the ionosphere, they start to glow. This is much the same way that electrons passing through the gases in a neon tube make a neon sign light up. It has been estimated that these solar winds can generate up to 100,000 megawatts of electricity in a three-hour exhibition. Unfortunately, these intense displays also cause troubling interference with power lines, radio and television broadcasts, and satellite communications.

It is also true that the dazzling lights on earth can interrupt our communications with God. *"Do not love the world or the things in the world. If anyone loves the world, the love of the Father is not in him" (1 John 2:15). "Now the ones that fell among thorns are those who, when they have heard, go out and are choked with cares, riches, and pleasures of life, and bring no fruit to maturity" (Luke 8:14).*

Placebo

An Effective Medicine

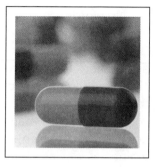

A placebo is a harmless pill or solution made from a neutral substance, such as sugar or saline, that is used to avoid bias when testing new drugs. But in some tests, patients have experienced dramatic results from these placebos based simply on their belief that the pill would help them.

Doctors have administered placebos to patients who are thought to have incurable illnesses to induce the so-called placebo effect: a temporary or even permanent improvement of the patient's condition that may correspond to their faith in the doctor or medicine they are given. In 1955, a study by Dr. Henry Knowles Beecher reported that the health condition of 60 percent of patients had improved by receiving placebos.

Little is understood of how this works, but one theory is that the patient's faith in a cure might be related to the release of brain chemicals that help promote healing. Perhaps this is why Jesus always said to those He healed, "Your faith has made you whole."

Modern medicine is returning to the conclusion that a person's faith has a great deal to do with their rate of recovery. In fact, one study reported that those who attend religious services more than once a week have a seven-year longer life expectancy than those who never attend.

The Bible also teaches that a person's eternal life expectancy is directly connected with their faith. *"Fight the good fight of faith, lay hold on eternal life"* (1 Timothy 6:12).

SynCardia

A Matter of the Heart

In June 2016, a young man in Michigan received a heart transplant. This is always a miraculous process, of course, but what made this case especially remarkable is that before the surgery, the patient lived for a year and a half without a human heart inside his body!

Stan Larkin, 25, had been diagnosed as a teenager with cardiomyopathy, a serious genetic heart condition. In 2014, he was admitted to the University of Michigan Cardiovascular Center in very frail condition and desperately in need of a heart transplant. The problem was that there were no adequate donor hearts available. So to buy him some precious time, the surgeons installed a device called "SynCardia." This sophisticated pump was powered by a 13-pound backpack holding batteries and a compressor that ran 24/7. This allowed Stan to be discharged from the hospital and live a semi-normal life, even playing a little basketball. Before his heart transplant, Stan lived 555 days outside the hospital without a human heart.

Did you know the Bible says that every true believer in God will experience a heart transplant? *"I will give you a new heart and put a new spirit within you; I will take the heart of stone out of your flesh and give you a heart of flesh. I will put My Spirit within you and cause you to walk in My statutes, and you will keep My judgments and do them" (Ezekiel 36:26, 27).*

Black Holes

A Bottomless Pit

Black holes are a unique phenomenon in space caused by objects with such concentrated mass that their immense gravitational pull sucks in light. For example, a star with ten times the mass of our sun would become a black hole if it were compressed to the size of New York City in diameter.

Stock photo illustration

The minimum speed required to escape Earth's gravitational pull is called the "escape velocity." Now imagine an object with a required escape velocity greater than the velocity of light—186,000 miles per second! Although no one has seen a black hole, scientists have observed objects around black holes and have made assumptions based on those observations.

The gravitational force of black holes is so strong that the laws of physics no longer apply in them. What causes matter to become so concentrated as to produce a black hole? It occurs when a star dies and the core continues to collapse, forming such a super dense mass that nothing can escape.

The Bible teaches us that when Lucifer fell, he imploded like a fallen star and refused to allow the light of truth to escape his domain. *"How you are fallen from heaven, O Lucifer, son of the morning! How you are cut down to the ground, you who weakened the nations!" (Isaiah 14:12).*

Carrington Super Flare

Fierce Solar Storm

In September 1859, the Carrington Super Flare—the largest solar flare in modern history—struck the earth, causing the most powerful geomagnetic storm ever recorded. For one thing, this made the Northern Lights so intense, they were visible to the Caribbean Islands. And they were so bright over the Rockies that many thought it was morning.

Stock photo illustration

As beautiful as it was, this solar storm also caused the failure of telegraph lines across Europe and North America. In an instant, the communication system upon which millions depended was fried. It is believed that if a solar flare of this scale hit the world today, it would wipe out the Internet and modern communications on a global scale.

The Bible says this would not be the first time international communications broke down due to a heavenly phenomenon. *"The LORD came down to see the city and the tower which the sons of men had built. And the LORD said, 'Indeed the people are one and they all have one language, and this is what they begin to do; now nothing that they propose to do will be withheld from them. Come, let Us go down and there confuse their language, that they may not understand one another's speech.' So the LORD scattered them abroad from there over the face of all the earth, and they ceased building the city. Therefore its name is called Babel, because there the LORD confused the language of all the earth; and from there the LORD scattered them abroad over the face of all the earth"* (Genesis 11:5–9).

SR-71 Blackbird

Bird of Prey

The first flight of Lockheed Aircraft's SR-71 "Blackbird" took place in 1964, and the plane officially entered military service in January 1966. For years, the Blackbird's maximum speed and altitude were kept top secret. But we now know that the aircraft set two world records for absolute speed (2,193 mph) and altitude (85,068 feet).

For more than thirty years, the SR-71 flew with impunity. With its cruising speed of Mach 3 and altitude, no missile or plane could catch it. As a result, despite hundreds of reconnaissance missions over hostile territory, not a single aircraft was lost to enemy fire.

The Blackbird could fly from Los Angeles to Washington, D.C. in one hour, surveying 100,000 square miles along the way! And it flew so fast that to refuel in-flight, the sleek jet had to fly as slow as possible and the refueling aircraft as fast as possible to keep from colliding.

While the capabilities of the steel bird have not been surpassed, the SR-71 was retired in 1990, although it saw temporary reinstatement during the Gulf War. It seems such a tragic waste of potential, power, and designing genius to have these wonders of the sky chained to the ground and rusting in museums.

But sadder still is when millions of people go through their lives chained to sin when God designed them to fly. *"Because the creation itself also will be delivered from the bondage of corruption into the glorious liberty of the children of God"* (Romans 8:21). *"Stand fast therefore in the liberty by which Christ has made us free, and do not be entangled again with a yoke of bondage"* (Galatians 5:1).

Super Glue
The Strongest Bind

Did you know that super glue was discovered by accident during WWII? Dr. Harry Coover and the scientists at Kodak were actually trying to make clear plastics for precision gun sights. The troublesome chemicals (cyanoacrylates) they were using kept sticking together so quickly that they were impossible to use for the project.

Nine years later, in 1951, Dr. Coover was supervising a project to develop a heat resistant polymer for jet canopies. One team member, Fred Joyner, spread some of the cyanoacrylate between a pair of refractor prisms. To his surprise, the prisms became stubbornly stuck together. This time, Dr. Coover realized the great commercial potential of a powerful adhesive that would quickly bond to a variety of materials. The product, eventually named Super Glue, really is "super." Just one-square-inch bonding of Super Glue can hold nearly a ton!

Perhaps today's marriages could use some super glue. Did you know the second chapter of the Bible says a husband and wife should be glued together? *"Therefore a man shall leave his father and mother and be joined [daw-bak' Hebrew: to cling or adhere to; to be joined; to keep (fast), stick] to his wife, and they shall become one flesh"* (Genesis 2:24).

Tsunamis
A Wall of Water

Tsunamis are among the most destructive natural disasters, in large part because a third of the world's population lives within sixty miles of the ocean. These sea waves are caused by earthquakes, undersea landslides, volcanic eruptions, or even asteroids striking the ocean—all of which result in a sudden colossal movement of seawater.

Stock photo illustration

Tsunamis can look like massive, towering waves or quickly rising monster tides that surge in without warning. Out in the deep ocean, a tsunami wave can travel at speeds greater than 500 mph—as fast as a jet plane! These killer waves are often only a foot high in the deep ocean and might not even be noticed by boats in the area, but as they reach shallow water, the waves grow much taller, some over 100 feet high!

Tsunamis can occur hundreds of times each year—a majority in the Pacific Ocean—although most are too small to notice. But every few years, a seismic event produces a large tsunami wave that kills thousands. For instance, the famous volcanic explosion of Krakatoa in 1883 generated terrifying tsunami waves up to 120 feet in height. These waves destroyed 165 towns and villages in Western Java and Southern Sumatra and killed over 36,000 people.

The largest tsunami wave ever recorded in modern times was in Lituya Bay, Alaska. This mega-tsunami was caused by a massive landslide triggered by a 7.8-magnitude earthquake. When the wave rushed across the bay, it ran up the valley walls to a height of 1,710 feet. And more recently, on December 26, 2004, more than 230,000 people in Southeast Asia lost their lives to a tsunami triggered by a 9.1-magnitude earthquake at the bottom of the ocean.

Did you know God promises to protect us from the spiritual tsunamis that endanger our souls? *"For this cause everyone who is godly shall pray to You in a time when You may be found; surely in a flood of great waters they shall not come near him"* (Psalm 32:6).

Stock photo illustration

The Black Death
A Plague of Biblical Proportions

The Black Death, a particularly nasty form of bubonic plague, has killed an estimated 75 million people since it first appeared in the fourteenth century. In most cases, victims infected by the bacterium suffer from fever, chills, fatigue, and painfully swollen lymph nodes. The plague acquired its name from another symptom: hemorrhages that turned black.

The Black Death has been traced to the Gobi Desert in the 1320s. By 1400, it invaded China, reducing its population by a third. It then followed trade routes to India, the Middle East, and into Europe. In Cairo, at the height of the epidemic, 7,000 people died each day.

In 1347, Eurasian nomads deliberately infected a European community with the disease. While laying siege to a Genoese trading post in the Crimea, the nomads lobbed plague-infected corpses into the town by catapult. The Genoese then inadvertently brought the disease to Sicily in a ship carrying infected rats. It swept through Sicily in 1347; North Africa, Italy, France, and Spain in 1348; Hungary, Austria, Switzerland, England, and Germany in 1349; and reached Scandinavia in 1350. Some 25 million Europeans were killed by the initial onslaught of the Black Death; whole villages were wiped out.

In its course, the Black Death carried away a greater proportion of the world's population than any other disease or war in history. It transformed European society, reducing its population by at least a third. At its peak, no medical shield could protect against the Black Death, but today antibiotics can improve the chances of survival.

Did you know that the Bible says we have all been infected by a black death called sin? Thankfully, there's a cure. *"If we confess our sins, He is faithful and just to forgive us our sins and to cleanse us from all unrighteousness"* (1 John 1:9).

Voyager Missions
Interstellar Spacecraft

Without question, the Voyager 1 and 2 spacecrafts are among the most successful scientific expeditions in history. First launched in 1977, and designed to last about five years, both crafts are still communicating with us some forty years later.

The Voyagers gave us our first close-up photos of the great planets of our solar system. They explored Jupiter, Saturn, Uranus, and Neptune, as well as a number of moons and asteroids. And just in case they encounter intelligent life, both Voyager 1 and 2 are carrying a gold record imprinted with photos and drawings, spoken greetings in many languages, music, and other earth sounds. However, any extraterrestrials would first have to figure out how to build a record player to hear it.

Both Voyager spacecraft have left our solar system and are traveling through interstellar space at more than 38,000 mph. Powered by a radioisotope thermoelectric generator, Voyager 1 may keep exploring space for another twenty years before its power finally runs out. Because they are over 13 billion miles from earth, it takes over 16 hours for scientists to receive data from these special spacecrafts.

On the other hand, the Bible says your prayers reach heaven instantly. *"For the eyes of the Lord are on the righteous, and His ears are open to their prayers"* (1 Peter 3:12).

Three Gorges Dam

A Colossal Feat

It is the epitome of a monumental project: a dam nearly one-and-a-half miles wide and more than 600 feet high, creating a reservoir hundreds of feet deep and longer than the state of Oregon. Moreover, this dam's hydropower turbines can create as much electricity as fifteen nuclear power plants.

In 1994, China began one of the largest construction projects in history, known as the Three Gorges Dam, to control the 3,950-mile Yangtze River, which is the third longest river in the world. This nine-year project created the world's largest dam and hydroelectric power plant and was completed in 2012 at a cost of $28 billion.

The dam provides significant benefits, including flood protection, such as the catastrophic Yangtze River flood in 1998 that resulted in 3,700 deaths, 15 million homeless, and $24 billion in economic loss. The reservoir enables 5,000-ton freighters to travel directly into the nation's interior, decreasing transportation costs and promoting regional economic development.

China's leaders call the dam the greatest engineering feat since the construction of the Great Wall, but to critics worldwide, it is a social and environmental disaster. It has destroyed 13 major cities, 140 smaller cities, and more than 1,000 villages. Ancient temples, burial grounds, and hundreds of archeological sites are lost under water. More than 900 factories were lost and 1.4 million people were forced to relocate. Also consider that roughly 400 million people live within the watershed of the Yangtze River. In the event the dam breaks, millions of people who live downstream could perish.

You might be surprised to know that the book of Revelation predicts that a dragon will send a great flood to try to destroy God's church. *"So the serpent spewed water out of his mouth like a flood after the woman, that he might cause her to be carried away by the flood. But the earth helped the woman, and the earth opened its mouth and swallowed up the flood which the dragon had spewed out of his mouth" (Revelation 12:15, 16).*

Ultra Deep Field

Peering into God's Creation

The sheer vastness of space is truly incomprehensible to the human brain. Here's one example: Back in 1996, for ten days astronomers pointed the Hubble Space Telescope into a part of the sky close to the Big Dipper that seemed utterly empty.

The little patch they focused on is no bigger than a grain of rice held out at arm's length. Yet 3,000 galaxies came into focus, producing one of the most profound and humbling images in all of human history—every single smear and dot was an entire galaxy, a fiery pinwheel of light, each containing hundreds of billions of stars.

Then, between 2004 and 2014, using much improved equipment, they did it again. This time, they aimed the telescope toward an empty spot in the constellation Orion. Over 10,000 galaxies appeared in that speck of space dubbed the Ultra Deep Field. This is the farthest we've ever seen into the universe. But as if all this were not incredible enough, astronomers now estimate that this vast universe we see is really only four percent of what is out there.

The immensity of space is mind-boggling, yet the Bible says that God counts all the stars and has a name for each one. *"He counts the number of the stars; He calls them all by name"* (Psalm 147:4).

Get Bible Truth in Your Pocket!

The New Amazing Facts Mobile App

The Amazing Facts App puts our best resources into your hands—ready to inform you and help you share the good news with others no matter where you go!

Features ...

- AFTV
- *Sabbath School Study Hour*
- *Amazing Facts with Doug Batchelor*
- *Bible Answers Live*
- 24/7 Internet Radio
- Free Book Library
- Plus, Study Guides, Weekly Blog, and more!

AMAZING FACTS

Available now for IOS and Android

 ▶ **DOWNLOAD TODAY!**